CRUSHING YOUR FIRST 365 DAYS AS A NEW PA

HOW TO AVOID EMBARRASSMENT, MAKE MORE MONEY, AND DOMINATE YOUR NEW CAREER AS A PHYSICIAN ASSISTANT!

ELIO STONE

COMMON GROUND PUBLISHING

CONTENTS

I have been blessed to know many inspiring souls over the years. Thank you all for being such wonderful teachers, and for being patient enough for me to be taught.

To my wife Jamie...only you know how much I have struggled, and only you have known how to bring in the light when there was darkness. I remain eternally grateful for you.

"Come to the edge, he said

We might fall, they said

Come to the edge, he said

It's too high, they said

Come to the edge, he said

And so they came

And he pushed them

And they flew."

— CHRISTOPHER LOGUE

INTRODUCTION

First and foremost, a tremendous congratulations for not only getting into PA school but graduating as well! If you have not graduated yet, relax! You are almost there! I know it's been a long twisty road, and it's very exciting to know you have made it this far! I'm sure you're well aware by this point that the PA profession and these programs have become increasingly popular over the last several years. This means that the precious few spots that were hard to get into *before*, have become extremely hard to get into *now*!

I know all too well the difficulty of getting into PA school...I struggled embarrassingly for years to get in before I was finally accepted. I am still thankful after all these years that one program director took a chance on me, and I made sure I didn't let her down (Professor Salzer, if you're reading this, thank you for changing my life). Trust me when I say this, I am intimately familiar with that struggle. I know if you made it this far, one thing is for sure...you've got grit!

A little bit about me, and why I am qualified to speak with you on the subject of being a PA. I have had over 25 years of "in the trenches" healthcare experience in various capacities...everything from Patient Transporter, ICU Nursing Assistant, ER Tech, EMT, and Mental Health Worker, to finally becoming a PA. It was a very long and bumpy road for me, but in the last 10 years or so I've worked exclusively in Orthopedic Surgery. Within my role in Orthopedics, I have practiced Orthopedic Trauma, Joint Replacement, Hand and Upper Extremity Surgery, and even some Sports and Spine. I have mentored PAs and PA students along the way, and have been involved with pre-college programs that help developing young minds gain exposure to the healthcare industry and all the moving parts.

With all of those very different experiences, I feel relatively well-rounded and well-suited to help you with some decision-making and mind-framing as you move forward during this wonderful time in your life. If you take some of my advice in this book, you too will build a solid foundation from which to grow. So, when a mangled limb or a complex medical patient walks into your office or ER, you won't panic and run for the nearest restroom. Instead, you'll know how to act decisively and confidently, wielding your formidable knowledge and wide breadth of skills to save the day!

While growing up in healthcare, I have gained a tremendous amount of insight from not only the patients but from the people I've worked with...the Physicians, the Nurses, the healthcare professionals, and everyone in between. While sometimes it did indeed feel a little like Grey's Anatomy, for the most part, I found the whole experience extremely humbling. I'll take a quick moment to say something very important here, and that is this...taking care of someone else is a privilege. They are inviting you into their lives, often unwillingly, to help them through difficulties in their life. They don't know you, and yet they have to open themselves up in an intimate way to you, which means they make themselves vulnerable to you. That vulnerability is granted with the assumption that you will do no harm, and in fact that you will care for them to the best of your capacity. Please remember this thing, because when the newness of your role wears off and things become routine, and patients become just another room number or chart, you will become numb to it. We are all guilty of it. But if you continue to honor it, that vulnerability that patients present to you will create some of the most transformative moments of your life. I can attest to that.

Think of this book then as a collage of experiences from one friend to another. Let's pretend we're at happy hour, and I'm trying to give you dating advice...we'll keep it light and fun (for the most part). However, I do want to make something abundantly clear from the start. I do NOT know it all about being a PA, and you may disagree with some of the things that I say. That's ok with me. We must all develop our own journey. I have walked my road in medicine, and now it is time for you to walk yours. I speak to you as someone who has made many, many mistakes in their medical career. Despite all those mistakes, I somehow survived to tell about it and continued to enjoy all the day-to-day trappings of being a PA, which has no doubt significantly molded me into the person I am today. May this professional sunrise you are now experiencing bring out the absolute best in you and in all whom you come to touch in life.

Welcome, my friends, to the real world of medicine.

1

WHERE TO CALL HOME

Before we get into it, some basic housecleaning. This book will not spend any time on the PANCE. There are plenty of wonderful preparatory texts for that purpose, and you should seek out those resources in earnest. I do, however, make a strong suggestion here in that you do NOT delay taking the PANCE. Some people feel after they complete the program like taking a vacation and blowing off some steam, which is absolutely OK and certainly warranted! By all means, after you graduate, take a week or two of vacation and decompress if you so wish, Jello shots are optional. Just make sure you have the PANCE scheduled in advance though, so that you stick to, and are accountable to, a timeline. Do not, and I reiterate, do NOT delay taking the PANCE longer than 4-6 weeks following graduation. I can't tell you how many times I have heard over the years what a mistake that was for some people.

For myself, I scheduled the PANCE to be taken 2 weeks after my graduation day. I decided I would take the boards and then vacate after. While this happened to be a very good strategy on my part, I did have a very close friend who thought that they were entitled to 6 weeks of vacation following their graduation. Those 6 weeks quickly turned into 2 months, and then into 12. You see, the information leaves you pretty rapidly when you're not using it. That person, unfortunately, had tremendous diffi-culty passing the PANCE after their "vacation", ulti-mately taking them over a year of no income before they became certified.

Will some people wait longer than 4-6 weeks and do fine? Of course! You have to know what kind of person you are, and only you can make that type of decision. If you gain nothing else from this book, then please just trust me on this one particular thing, and take the boards as quickly as you can after you graduate. Stick to your timeline, don't delay. Besides, you should have been studying for your boards during your rotations in the second half of your program. So, by the time you're ready to take the boards, you've been in essence studying for over a year for it, and at this point just need a brief review to rock the exam! Right?! Now that we have that little bit of business out of the way, let's get on with it.

I'll venture a guess that most of you have known for a long time that you would eventually end up in medicine. Perhaps some of you had a toy stethoscope growing up, and you played Doctor with your sibling or the kid next door. Enamored with fixing the bumps and the bruises, you imagined yourself saving the day and being a hero to your patient when they fell from their bike and skinned a knee! Perhaps some of you were drawn to a certain lifestyle or salary, and perhaps some others just knew they wanted to wear a white lab coat. Show of hands...who knew that they *always* wanted to be a PA? <cue tumbleweed> Whatever your initiation to medicine was, I'm sure most, if not all of us, did not grow up wanting to be a PA. We didn't even know what that was! We wanted to be Doctors, of course!

I was well into my pre-med program at University before I even heard the term "Physician Assistant"... and to this day I'm not entirely sure how I did initially hear of it. As far as I was concerned at that point in my life, I was heading to med school. But when I discovered the benefits of the PA profession, I set my sights on that and didn't look back. The point is that most of us have been drawn to medicine in one way or another, but not necessarily to life as a PA. Look, it's ok if you wanted to be a Doctor, but chose to be a PA. We all have our reasons for being here, and they are all very good reasons! You did not choose 2nd best by choosing to be a PA. I'm here to tell you that you made an excellent decision to go to PA school and that it's a wonderful profession to devote yourself to! So if you had any residual feelings of inferiority by choosing team PA, LET THEM GO, now. Drop them like you would a lump of hot coal, and realize you have chosen wisely!

As for me, I can't remember a time when I didn't want to work in a hospital. My mother worked for years as a floor assistant at a large inner-city hospital near our home in Suburbia. I remember visiting mom at work and being smitten with the small city feel of the huge place, the vastness of it, and all the different people buzzing about there...so many things happening all the time! When I turned 14, I was old enough to volunteer there, so I did! For 2 years, I performed various tasks through the volunteer department such as greeting patients, collecting wheelchairs, and directing patients to testing centers...the work was not hard, but I was 100% hooked. I loved being in the hospital environment, there was always excitement in the air. There were folks in scrubs, some in suits, and everything in between. And of course, there were patients everywhere. All of this together made for a very entertaining place to be for me, and I just felt that it was the place for me. This informal introduction to a slice of the healthcare pie made an indelible mark on me, and I was belly up at the counter for more.

Of all the many departments I was exposed to while working in the hospital, Orthopedics intrigued me the most, by far. I'm a very tactile learner, so seeing and feeling things help me to understand them. The son of a gifted mechanic, I was raised with a firm mechanical approach to fixing things, and an abundance of tools was always around me. I would routinely help my father fix cars or maintain mechanical things...I loved the feel of actually fixing something with tools. The musculoskeletal system, and the tools and hardware used to fix it, just made sense to me...it was a natural professional segue from my youth. And come on, as one of my former professors would say, "surgery is sexy!!" I knew it was going to be Orthopedic Surgery for me or it was going to be nothing at all. So when I entered the PA program, I essentially had blinders on for Ortho, but I had the where-with-all to pay attention to everything.

I'm so thankful for this because little did I know how important all of that education you have just received would come to be. Turns out, it's not all "bone broke, me fix", after all...even in Ortho! You have just experienced the expression that PA school is like trying to take a sip from a fire hydrant, there is so much information! Well, I got news for you, the water pressure gets kicked up a couple of notches once you start your new practice! Not only do you have to have all the complex medicine stuff figured out, but then there are all the other things associated with starting a new job...the logistics, the software, the other professionals you're working with, scheduling, benefits, CMEs, your favorite parking spot, and (usually) safe toilet...there is just so much! And, on top of that, you'll be surprised to know that there are some really smart people practicing medicine! You have to know enough to be able to engage these people at a high enough level so that they don't think you're a total waste of space!

Why I am telling you all this? Because I don't want you to have any additional stress in your life at this point in time... there will be plenty of time for stress when practicing medicine! Right now we need to be clear on your future career path in medicine...what will you be doing? To be certain, when you have the presence of mind and clarity in your decision-making, you will have minimal stress and you will act with the confidence of a professional. It might not be as easy as "I've always wanted to do Ortho" like it was for me. However, If you have been deliberately avoiding deciding on your future after graduation, it is time to get off the fence guys. We need you to pick an area of medicine to work.

If you're having trouble deciding, take a walk in the woods, meditate, sage yourself, or whatever works for you... we just need to get closer to deciding on what kind of medicine to practice. Once you have it, stop debating, commit, and move forward! Do not get stuck in analysis paralysis, weighing the pros and cons of different specialties. Yes, they each do have their pros and cons of course, but most of them you won't be able to appreciate until you've been in practice for quite some time anyways! Remember, you can't get started on anything meaningful until you make a decision, so we need to decide, preferably today!

I know...you're asking yourself "How can he possibly ask me to make this huge decision on my future right now??" I understand, there is much to consider...been there. If you're worried about making the wrong decision, that's OK! Accept the fact that you might! How can you possibly know that you will love a certain practice of medicine after spending a few incredibly short weeks there during your rotations? Look, you may pick wrong...so what? You're not going to know that definitively until you immerse yourself and give it at least 6 months to a year...you owe yourself at least that. If at that time it's a bust, you can change things up. A word of caution, however, because this is one of the first few places that people start to go wrong. After being (really) broke and hungry and tired for the last several years, you are likely extremely eager to start making some good money. What some new grads do at this point is to take the first job they can find where they can make the most amount of money, regardless of what field it's in.

For example, Urgent Care positions tend to be low-hanging fruit for PAs in that they pay well, offer shift work, and typically have employment opportunities. However, Physician oversight and collaboration in Urgent Care centers tends to be nonexistent, there is often a very high expectation of increased throughput and seeing as many patients as you can in a short amount of time. Although the money would be good, you don't have the experience necessary to properly evaluate each patient, and you know that. Since each patient would likely cause you to struggle, you'd have a major increased level of stress in your life, decreased job satisfaction, and ultimately get burned out. You'd be done before even getting started. I know, because I have seen this play out time and time again. So, while there are great opportunities for jobs making great money right off the bat, it may not be a great fit for a new grad. More on that to follow.

So, take some time and decide on an area of medicine to work in. Once that is done, we can start job hunting! When I graduated from my PA program, PA jobs were still very plentiful, and you had your pick of quite a few openings at any given time because demand was so incredibly high. Over the last few years, and especially post-pandemic when there have been restrictions on hiring, the positions have been harder to find, there is no doubt about it. Usually, the available positions typically require some baseline level of experience, which as a new grad is obviously a limiting issue. How do we combat the need for some income in a very competitive job market, with no professional experience you ask? Well, the key is in being flexible and dynamic. When you first graduate from PA school, you are unlikely to get your "dream job". There, I said it. This did not happen for me, and it will likely not happen for you. However, there are some basics you can stick to which can subsequently be applied to later choices in your career that will help you go farther, faster.

Let's say you were like me and had a craving to work in Orthopedic Surgery after school. You search and search and search for Orthopedic Surgery opportunities for new grad PAs, and there are just none to be had. Bummer! Looks like you'll be living in mom and dads basement for a little longer. I mean, mom buys that nice fabric softener and she keeps snacks in the pantry, so it's not so bad, right? *Wrong!* You're moving out! Let's say instead of finding one of those coveted Orthopedic Surgery jobs, you see several openings for a new grad in Colorectal Surgery. While seemingly not so glamorous in your initial assessment, that specialty does open you up to the world of both inpatient and outpatient surgical practice, and would also give you a baseline level of comfort managing post-surgical patients as well as the variety of situations faced in an operating room on a routine basis. These skills could later be applied to other surgical subspecialties, like Orthopedics or Plastics. You would subsequently gain as much experience as you could or were comfortable with, and then move on once your ideal opportunity came along.

The point is not to focus on the money or the particular specialty when you graduate but instead focus on the skills that you will be obtaining and utilizing in the future. It's all about those skills guys! Those are the things that will make you marketable and attractive to employers moving forward! More skills = more money! New grads always want to do what's sexy and exciting, but you may have to do something a little more down-to-earth until you build up your chops! Keeping a very open mind after graduation and not allowing yourself to become frustrated when you can't find the exact perfect job allows you to work towards your more ideal position once you've gotten some experience under your belt.

While this may seem like common knowledge, I hear it from new grads all the time about them holding out for better positions. Forget that nonsense! The most important thing you can do after you graduate is to start working! You need to make money, you need to gain experience! Please do not sit around waiting for the right opportunity to come along, because I assure you it will be scooped up by someone else. 12,000 PAs are graduating in this country annually, which means that 12,000 other people are looking for work just like you! And it will be your skill set and level of experience that makes you marketable above your peers moving forward. Again, if you're anything like me after graduation, you are likely darn near broke and very eager to start working...so don't just see the specialty, see the skills and the experience you'll acquire. You'll thank me later!

The other thing to consider is that those skills that will get you better paid in the long run do not come cheap. You have to put your time in, and that makes some people very uncomfortable. Let me give you an example of what I'm talking about. A dear friend of mine graduated from an anesthesia program and did quite well academically. After they graduated, they found a cozy position that paid very well and had an easy schedule at a small outpatient surgery practice. This was seemingly a gigantic win. However, the problem with this approach being fresh out of school is that because it was a small tertiary medical center, this person would have much less exposure to more intense situations than they may have found in a larger teaching center or city location.

Now don't get me wrong, we absolutely should be serving rural and outlying communities with our medical care, indeed that's where our profession excels. However, out of school, you cannot serve those people to the best of your ability in those communities unless you know what you are doing, because supervision and collaboration with Physician leadership would likely be limited or nonexistent. The whole idea of Physician extension is built on the premise that we go where they are not. I don't know about you, but I don't like to be scared or intimidated by difficult patient situations. Even after 10 years of on-call Orthopedics, there are still surprises. If it happens to be 2 am and you're on call when that difficult patient situation comes up, you will know how to handle it if you have the right skill set. You might not ever develop that skill set working a cushy job right out of school that is not very demanding and does little to develop you professionally.

"But wait, Elio, I don't care about any of that", you say. "I just want to find a job." That's fine my friend, just know that this is medicine. Medicine has a long-standing hierarchy, as you are all well aware of by this point. If you want to be respected and paid well for what you do, you need to develop the skills and have the information to deliver. So you can get paid well and be mediocre, or you can be paid even better and be awesome. Another way of looking at is do you just want to collect a paycheck and be fearful when the tough patient comes across your door, or do you want to make bank and be a rockstar PA hero when you get that 2 am ER call? Your choice.

If you're still struggling, and you're having a hard time just keeping it basic and choosing between medicine versus surgery, take the following with a grain of salt. In the real world, medicine and surgery approach problems from very different perspectives, and you for sure gained some exposure to some of this on your rotations. Surgeons are typically more mechanical and have a desire and the capability to fix problems more acutely. In the medicine world, most will agree that there is a more cerebral approach to discovering and treating problems, and often times medicine and surgery are at odds. This different approach to treating problems sometimes creates a playful and interesting relationship between medical and surgical colleagues.

In my world of Orthopedics, we are typically seen as the "dumb jocks" who just want to cut. While many of us in Orthopedics do tend to keep in good shape, it's also true that Orthopedic residencies are some of the most challenging and intense residencies to not only be accepted into but to also complete. It's been my experience that Orthopedic residents are some of the highest-performing residents on the medical spectrum. So, I've heard plenty of jokes over the years about being a dummy in Orthopedics, while my medical colleagues laugh at my attempts at medical management. But I certainly don't laugh at them when they turn pale and have a Vagal event as they watch us perform a fracture manipulation. I also don't laugh when they go running for an emesis basin while I deal with that ER patient that has a hand that's been terribly mangled from being stuck in a snowblower.

The point is, that the two worlds are pretty different, and they attract very different personalities. In the surgical world, we are typically up pretty early and are rounding often before 6 am because surgical cases will often start churning just after 7 am. That means you have to have all of your ducks in a row before disappearing into the OR for the day. Also, you tend to live in scrubs. Naturally, surgical subspecialties and their scheduling tend to be a little bit more inconsistent, unpredictable, and more acute in nature. Sometimes, you really are running to the OR for that acute patient management! This is a very different world than medicine, where you may have noticed there is not so much sudden action and acuity in their day, aside from the occasional code. In my career, I have often observed medicine strolling leisurely onto the floor and starting their day rounding around 9 am, after having tossed back their Starbucks. Of course, this is different in the

ICU where medical management is at its most intense, but you get the point...they are different worlds.

So again, as we mentioned previously, you have to know what kind of person you are. Do you see yourself as fairly rigid, with difficulty in sudden transitions, or in more acute situations that can be more intense? If that's the case, you may prefer a more structured day in medicine as opposed to surgery, where the schedule and routine of things tend to be more consistent. If you do prefer less rigidity in your day, more variability, higher acuity at times, and often much more adrenaline, a surgical specialty may be what you need. Either way, you can have a very successful and rewarding career if what you choose fits your personality and lifestyle. And again, we are speaking in terms of generalizations here, and keeping it pretty casual. Of course, there are medical specialties that are very intense and acute in nature, and there are some very sedate surgical specialties that have a very consistent schedule. On the whole, however, the differences we noted tend to be pretty universal across healthcare.

I'll mention one final thing here about choosing a medical or surgical specialty. In terms of going with surgery (and hopefully, this isn't a shocker) but you'll have to be working alongside surgeons. As you have likely appreciated from your rotations, most surgeons tend to carry reputations that label them as difficult to work with. Is that all of them? Of course not! I have known some very laid-back and peaceful surgeons in my day. However, the overwhelming majority of them have been intense, demanding, at times irrational, and with a predilection for egocentricity. The "God-complex", as we sometimes hear being joked around with. Dealing with surgeons and their level of intensity can be exhausting, and very humbling. When you do it day in and day out, you can find yourself becoming increasingly frustrated with them and your work.

This certainly happened to me initially in my career, but then I quickly learned that these people have a tremendous amount of responsibility and stress to deal with when they decide to operate. It doesn't excuse them from being jerks sometimes, but it did help me keep things in perspective in that their job is extremely difficult. Now, that doesn't mean I let myself get walked on, but I have learned to let a lot of things go and not take it all personally. Frankly, if I had the level of responsibility that they did at times,

I would be a little bit worked up as well. Just know that surgeons will add another layer of complexity to your work, so if you are the type that is easily offended, don't bother getting into surgical practice. Especially Orthopedics!!

2

THE HUNT FOR A JOB

Before we start talking about actually finding a job, we need to discuss the term "mid-level provider", because you may see this ridiculous descriptor while job hunting, or you may have been exposed to it during your rotations. Please, please, do not ever refer to yourself as a mid-level provider. There is nothing mid-level about a Physician Assistant! I understand that it has become political and academic to utilize certain terms to help categorize different trends in healthcare, but the interpretation of a mid-level provider is that you're somewhere between a Doctor and a Nurse. This is absolutely not the case.

You are a healthcare professional, trained in the medical model, and utilizing terms such as a mid-level provider does not help elevate our profession. Be mindful of these things moving forward. The other issue with that term is the implication that you are less than something but more than something else. In the landscape of healthcare, we are on a gigantic team all together. I know this sounds cliché, but only when the team works together do we have successful outcomes for our patients.

There will be much more on interacting with teams and other professionals within the healthcare landscape later, but I wanted to introduce that here now as you will likely see that term as you seek employment. Some of the more modern terms I have been exposed to recently are "Physician Extenders", and "Advanced Practice Providers". Increasingly, I just see the blanket term "Provider" being utilized, which I think is fair and accurate. Some of these descriptors will also vary greatly depending on where you live, and the local customs of your healthcare organizations. Whatever the case may be, remember that your chosen profession is still relatively young, and we continue to carve out our place in healthcare every single day. When we accept professional labeling that is neither accurate nor promotional, we dilute our collective years of training and hard work. Remember to always be elevating your profession!

So now that we have our mindset about an area of medicine to call home for at least a little while, let's talk about how we can actually find a job. One of the lessons I learned early on when I was fresh out of school was the concept of leverage...having other people help you to perform a task so that you can multiply your efforts. You see, I had no pull in medicine when I graduated. No Cardiologist uncle, no Nurse aunt, no Xray Tech cousin...nobody. Yes, my mom worked at a hospital, but she didn't have any influence at that level. Since I didn't have much professional pull with my local healthcare organizations, I looked for help.

You may not be aware of these folks yet, but healthcare recruiters are people who search and shop job opportunities for you, once you've told them a little bit about what your specific goals are. The great thing is, you do not pay these people...that is a common misconception. They are paid by the hiring organizations once the position is filled with a suitable candidate. Therefore, as you are looking for a job, you can leverage several other recruiters to look for positions for you as well, seriously amping up your job-finding efforts. Good healthcare recruiters are heavily connected in the space, they have their feelers out in different organizations, and they are usually aware of potential job openings before they become public knowledge. I'm reluctant to mention some recruiter names here because they can be quite regional and specific to the areas that they serve. However, depending on where in the country you happen to be located, if you search for health-care recruiters (hopefully ones that work specifically with PAs), you should come up with at least a handful of recruiters who are working your local job market. With all of you working on the same goal, you would theoretically have an easier time nailing down employment opportunities.

That does not mean you sit back and relax during the process! Quite the contrary, you have to aggressively shop for employment opportunities once you graduate, and this process can start before you've even taken the boards. These days, I hear all the time of people accepting positions with certain organizations under the condition that they will take and pass their boards within a certain allotted time frame. This might be a great benefit, as it motivates you to get the boards out-of-the-way, so you can start making some money. So, search and reach out to these folks, they can be a tremendous time saver. In fact, my first job out of school was found for me by a local healthcare recruiter, and the position wasn't even posted until after I applied. So, give them a try!

Then of course there are the usual job boards and job posting services, like ZipRecruiter, Indeed, and others. These can be a one-stop shop for some folks, but I have always found that being more proactive with the job search typically yields more positive results. So one tactic I used later in my career when I was ready for a change was to search specific healthcare organizations for their job postings. If they had opportunities I was interested in, or I felt I might be interested in the future, I would find the Human Resources contacts for those organizations on LinkedIn, and initiate some conversation about employment opportunities and my desire for a position within their organization. After breaking the ice, I would start submitting applications for positions while keeping an open line of communication with HR personnel through LinkedIn. Don't spam them for crying out loud! Just check in with them periodically, no more than weekly.

I know I'm not the first person to utilize this strategy, and there certainly are other resources available to discuss that in detail, but the point is to be proactive and to reach out to people in the areas of medicine you wish to work in, even if they don't currently have an opening for employment. You want them to know your name and think of you when they *do* have an opening because likely that time will come. I applied with one organization 6 different times for the same job, and I believe that my relationship with the HR personnel over LinkedIn, and them seeing my application on a regular consistent basis, made them grab my application when the next opportunity came along in a very competitive Orthopedic Surgery practice. So if you don't yet have a LinkedIn profile, get to it. If you do, make sure it's updated. This goes without saying guys, keep it clean and professional.

Now I'm going to get a little personal for a minute about the socials since I've mentioned LinkedIn. If you don't think HR departments and hiring offices will Google you or look up your Facebook and Instagram profiles, you're wrong. They absolutely will, and they are doing it more and more these days. I have connections in HR departments within large healthcare and insurance systems, and it's common practice in 2022 for you to be "researched" before a job offer. Especially for a high-paying, direct patient interaction type of role as a PA.

So, BEFORE you start seeking employment, clean it up, please. I know, I know...what happens in your private life is private, I respect that 100%. However, the fact is that questionable or illicit type activity documented on your socials may cause employers to view you as a liability, passing you up for someone else. Remember, it costs employers some serious money to get you onboarded. Credentialing, insurance, training, etc....employers spend big bucks and typically bare all the cost of you starting up until you are billing and making money for them. So, they are investing in you. They will be less willing to invest in you if they see you as reckless and untrustworthy. And, guess what? Patients will Google you too! They will seek you out on FB and IG. I also have socials, so I get it. I recently met with a new patient for a hand injury, and as I sat down with her, after a brief friendly greeting, she told me I have a beautiful family and that my son looks like my wife. She also asked me if we enjoyed the winery we went to the weekend before. OK, WHAT??! Ok, guys...it's extremely creepy and alarming when someone you weren't even aware existed a few moments ago knows that much about your life. Now she may have just been a casual FB "stalker", but you get the point. People will find you there, they will see what you post, and they will engage you on it. Food for thought.

If that wasn't enough, employers (especially larger systems), are enforcing policies on what material they deem appropriate for employees to post on their socials. They may make you sign an acknowledgment or waiver because frankly, they don't want bad publicity for their organization. I have unfortunately seen good people lose their jobs because of social media activity. This is not the place to discuss the politics of our freedom of speech, just know it's happening and I want you guys to be hyperaware of it. You've been warned, don't be careless and cavalier with your license, you've worked extremely hard for it!

From my humble perspective, probably the most important piece of the new job jigsaw puzzle would be what the Physician-PA relationship looked like. When I was in training, I had a rotation at a small tertiary hospital for General Surgery. While not a very large facility, it was extremely busy. One of the PAs I was assigned to for shadowing was very intimidating. He didn't speak much to me, and on top of that, he was physically a very large person, usually too much in a hurry to discuss much of anything with the students. One day, we happened to be sitting in the cafeteria together at the same table. I did not have much rapport with him up until this point, so I struck up the nerve to break the uneasy silence at the table. It was clear from rounds that the other Physicians respected his medical opinions, and I admired that. So, I asked him a question about what I thought would lead to some great conversation, and that is what his relationship with our supervising Physician (ie - his boss) was like. He calmly put down his fork, looked up at me with a glazed look of confusion, and told me he had no idea what I was referring to. He then picked his fork back up and resumed eating as if no question had ever been asked. We subsequently finished lunch in silence, and he went about the rest of his day. True story.

This was a very peculiar interaction for me because I thought that every PA had a solid working relationship with their supervising Physician, but what I learned from him that day is that often this notion of supervising Physician is one on paper, and not in practice. This absolutely does not mean that the relationship is not essential, quite the contrary, it's foundational to our practice in medicine. What I mean to say is that some PAs simply view the relationship as a formality. This particular PA had about two decades of experience on me, and it was pretty clear that he felt more than comfortable and confident in his role to not require much Physician oversight if any at all. And you know what? After two decades in medicine, he deserved some of that.

However, for the new grad, some sort of relationship with the supervising Physician is essential. You need to know who your supervising Physician will be, and what impact they will have on your day-to-day life. For some PAs in certain practices, you will never see the attending Physician, but they may be available by text...sometimes not even that. Like when they are 47 hours away out heli-skiing Whistler while "on-call" instead of being in the trauma room with you and that open Tibia (another true story)! In other practices, you are working side-by-side in the clinics with them, and they have 100% say in patient management. And somewhere in between are the rest of the PAs out there. The point is, as a new grad this relationship is important for you to have, and you need to have the right person interacting with you. We will discuss this at length a little later on because it's so incredibly important that we get it right.

We should also address this concept of "lateral flexibility" that we as PAs are all familiar with while we are job hunting. Now one of the biggest benefits of being a PA is that you are not tied to a particular specialty or practice of medicine. Physicians on the other hand, after undergoing residency and likely fellowship training, won't have the time or the ability to simply change gears after they've already developed a practice and patient following. Not only has all that been extremely expensive for them, but it's also been very time-consuming. The thought of undergoing another residency and possible fellowship is exhausting just to think about.

Therefore, once Physicians complete their residencies and fellowships, they are most likely married to that career until they retire. For PAs, there is the option to switch things up a bit and move into other specialties. This at first glance appears to be extremely convenient, and the thought of not being stuck in one area of medicine for the rest of your life is quite appealing. In practice, however, this becomes a very different reality. You see, once you begin working in your chosen field of medicine, you will strongly desire to be knowledgeable and very good at what you do. Why? Well, the real answer to that is because medicine is so fickle.

On my very first clinical rotation in PA school, I was at a large teaching facility in New York City, and I was very bright-eyed and full of excitement. On my second day of the rotation, I met the Medical Director, who was also the supervising Physician for the PA I was shadowing for that rotation. He was a very nice guy, obviously knowledgeable, and had worked extremely hard to obtain his current position and status. I remember we were standing at the counter in front of a patient room, and I was preparing to present a straightforward patient to my mentor when he stopped me and asked "Are you ready for all this?"

Well, I assumed he was referring to discussing the patient, so I of course nodded yes. Knowing that I didn't quite understand the question, he smiled and said "Look around". And so I did, looking at all the other professionals around me, the staff, the starched uniforms and the charts, the halls of patient rooms... and what he said next I'll never forget. He said "Are you ready to be judged on being you? Are you ready to be judged about how you dress, the way you are, how you write your charts, how you talk?" He asked me this because he knew that medicine was not a judgment-free zone and that at times the criticism can be extremely harsh. In essence, you must have thick skin to have success in medicine, because the criticisms will come whether you want them or not.

What I quickly came to realize after that exchange is that information really is powerful. I didn't want to be criticized for not knowing things, not knowing what to do or what to say. In my mind, the only way to avoid at least some of that criticism was to know the information. What does that mean? It means having as good or similar a level of understanding in that area of medicine as my supervising Physicians. If I didn't know, it was my job to find out.

I tell you all this because when you're out there in the real world and you are practicing medicine day in and day out, you will not want to feel like a fraud. You don't want to be a phony. You don't want patients to think you are incompetent with their care. You want them to think, "Wow, this person knows their stuff, and I feel 100% comfortable with them taking care of me! In fact, I would rather see them than the Physician!" But to obtain that kind of praise from your patients, you have to earn it.

Once you put the time and effort into mastering your craft in this manner, it's going to be challenging to restart all that somewhere else in medicine, learning and doing all those things over again. Not only did it take a long time to amass that knowledge and experience, but with it came frustration, the fear of uncertainty, and being new at something...it was uncomfortable for a while, growth always is. The point is, it's not going to be easy to change directions once you are good at what you are doing. Does that mean it's not possible? Of course not, I know PAs who have successfully accomplished this in medicine. Would I say that's the norm? Absolutely not. In my experience, practically speaking, it's much more reasonable to suggest that once you pick an area of medicine and a career, you will likely be committed. And that's OK! This of course does not mean that you might not want to change things up within your chosen focus.

For example, I did inpatient Orthopedics for a long time, but after getting tired of the call and brutal hospital hours, I switched to doing Orthopedics at an outpatient private office, where the hours and workload were more manageable. Still doing Orthopedics, just a little bit differently. And that, you will find, is actually a very common practice. Not only do I think this helps alleviate some overall healthcare burden, and healthcare provider burnout, but I am a huge proponent of continuing to reevaluate your life so that you can obtain an even better outcome for you and your family. If you get into a practice and after 6 months you feel like you're drowning, don't hesitate to get moving. You owe it to yourself after coming this far to continue to push higher not only for yourself but for your career. And if moving practices or changing your particular area of practice will benefit you in some way over the long run, go ahead and make the change.

I say all of this because I don't want you to enter into practice and in the back of your mind say to yourself "I'm not worried about what happens here the next few months because I can jump ship and do the next thing if I so choose." While yes that is technically true, remember that in practice it ends up being more difficult to make these kinds of changes, especially the longer you have been in one particular field. Also, please understand that reputation follows you around in healthcare.

Medical circles are not that large guys, and people frequently know one another and their reputations, especially at the local healthcare level. That means that people will know if you have burnt bridges or what kind of Provider you are once you have established yourself. There are plenty of PAs out there who hop around from job to job, seeking the next higher paycheck. I would suggest that not be you, because not only does it permanently damage your credibility, but it leaves a bad taste in the mouth of all the organizations that bothered to hire you. Burn too many bridges, and finding work for yourself in the future might become that much more challenging.

Also, we circle back to the notion of elevating the profession. You may be one of those folks that think solely about their own needs, and how much money you can make. That's fine, but for the rest of us who are in this to win it long-term, understand that the more you are seen as a trustworthy team player who takes excellent care of patients, the more lucrative the opportunities become as your career advances. You'll be surprised how others will seek you out and entice you with better opportunities, once they know you are someone that practices quality over quantity. You will find without question that more doors will start to open for you if have a long-term vision and commit yourself to do the best job you can where you're at. You've probably heard the expression, bloom where you're planted! Since we have broached the topic of reputation, let's talk more about that.

Stress and embarrassment are two things that most new grads will encounter, and indeed even as we mature along in our careers, we will have to deal with these things from time to time. How you decrease levels of stress and embarrassment, especially as a new grad, is to be properly informed. It's painfully simple. You have just embarked on a career that will require lifelong learning. Please reread that last bit guys, lifelong learning. If you are not committed to lifelong learning, please don't get started. I'm quite serious when I say that, do not continue further down this road if you will not commit yourself to learning.

Newsflash, once you graduate from PA school, you will only have a fraction of the knowledge that is required of you to succeed in your day-to-day life as a PA. The only way to fill in those gaps is to continue to learn and study the topics and cases you are presented with every single day in your career. Remember, we are trained in the medical model like our Physician counterparts. Physicians are at the top of the food chain in healthcare because they have the knowledge...not only did they commit themselves to a residency and often times fellowship, but they continue to educate themselves with collaboration and coursework throughout their careers. We are to take a page from their book.

No one will hold you accountable for your education more than your patients. Your patients will never ask you if you went home last night and read up on a case or procedure or topic that you were challenged with the day before. But they will assume that at this level of your career, you are consistently and effectively educating yourself regularly, especially when they know you are fresh out of training. The fact is, you will quickly see that the more knowledge you gain, the less stress your days will contain. The more knowledge about the specialty you're in, the more confidence when you are discussing treatments with patients. And when you are confident, patients receive that confidence and equate that with trust-worthiness, they will want you to take care of them.

I know what you're thinking..."Elio, if I just hunker down and study regularly, pouring into my career with knowledge, will I avoid all embarrassment my first year?" No, you likely won't. But I can tell you that you will save yourself a tremendous amount of grief and heartache if you remain humble and keep a positive attitude, remembering to ask questions when you're unsure. If you do these things, the patients and other staff will find your presence irre-sistible.

You do not have the privilege of having MD after your name, so you'll have to work a little harder to earn people's respect and trust in you. And honestly, that's OK. So that when you do make mistakes, and you have taken my advice, people will be much more willing to overlook those errors in judgment and continue to see you in a favorable light because they know you're genuine. They know that you really are doing your best and you're working from the heart. The wonderful thing about authenticity is that you never have to worry about what someone is going to find out about you. So be authentic, be genuine, be kind. In this instant gratification society and lifestyle that we all are now accustomed to, I know that once you graduate and the PANCE is in the rearview, you will see bucket loads of cashola in your future, and maybe a new BMW in your driveway. While these things may happen, and you are deserving of them, it does not give you the right to be an elitist or a jerk because you now have the letters PA-C after your name.

If I'm harping on this, it's because I know that when people become overconfident and cavalier, bad things can happen. That is a recipe for disaster for a patient, and I have seen my fair share of unfortunate and avoidable patient outcomes secondary to a provider with a short mindset and an ego the size of the Mississippi. Don't be that ego, because mistakes happen in medicine either way. If the mistake happens and it's a genuine mistake, you'll eventually forgive yourself as will those around you. But if you hurt someone because you were being careless, your career may be over. See the difference?

Now then, I'm going to give you my personal opinion on an ideal position for a new grad. This is strictly my opinion, so please don't roast me with your disagreements! I have come to have this opinion from years in the field and watching many PAs move through their careers during that time, some successfully, some unsuccessfully. Of course, it's not the only pathway, and other people may have even better ideas on this, but this is my perspective. And frankly, I feel it's the right one...

Whether you decide on medicine or surgery, as a new grad it's for your ultimate benefit that you look for a position where you are not a one-man show, and in fact, are surrounded by a team of high-caliber PAs who will help foster good habits and good knowledge within you. This is the fast track to success as a PA! You need a strong foundation to feel comfortable more quickly and demand higher salaries later in your career. I'm not going to sugar-coat it, the more you lower and humble yourself the first year, the more quickly you will develop the skills and knowledge to do more in medicine. When you're on a team, this does mean you at times have to eat humble pie. I know, I know. You have just spent the last year doing scut work as the full-time intern on your rotations, but now you will be getting paid handsomely for that scut work!

I strongly believe that a rewarding career in medicine depends upon the ability to develop critical knowledge and skills, while maintaining a humble and calm demeanor in oftentimes adverse situations. Some of you may say that the only job they can find right now is Urgent Care work or something similar to that... I understand. In that situation, look to see that when you're on shift, you're not the only PA. There needs to be other PAs to bounce ideas off of or maybe even a collaborating Physician you can ask questions of because those questions will most certainly come up during your first year. And if you don't have a way to address these questions in real-time with patients in the room, you're going to have a difficult time getting through each and every day. This is why I suggest strongly that you seek to find positions where there is more of a team-based practice mentality, it will pay dividends for you in the future.

A good example of this would be my very first job out of PA school. As I said before, I was hired by a tertiary healthcare organization at that time, and there were a handful of PAs that were working in Orthopedics at that particular location. There were some really good folks working there, and I did feel that I had a significant amount of support as a new grad. However, I was frequently on shift by myself even though several PAs were working in the department. The schedule was set up so that typically one or two PAs were on during the day, and then the remaining PAs were either scheduled for evenings or weekend coverage. What this effectively meant was that ER consults and floor issues were being managed and triaged by a new grad with minimal supervision.

Imagine a senior ER Physician pages you to the ER for a distal radius fracture he would like for you to manage, and you have never even pulled on a broken wrist before. He is the Physician, deferring to you the PA, and you have no idea what you are doing. While I did have some backup coverage in these situations, I definitely did not feel supported enough to take Orthopedic Trauma call as a new grad. Even though that was not a terribly busy service, it was busy enough and created enough stress and anxiety for me that I considered looking for alternative employment after just nine months. So even though there was a team in place at this particular organization, in practicality I was running solo much of the time.

Having become wise to the importance of support as a new grad, I joined a much larger PA team at a teaching facility for my next job. As I mentioned previously, there were about 10 to 15 PAs employed in the Orthopedic service at that organization, which meant that there were multiple PAs available most of the time to help me with issues that arose whether on the floor or in the ER. In fact, it would be highly unlikely for me to be attempting fracture care or dislocation reduction by myself, there was always a team member there to help. This was a much more supportive environment in terms of education, even though the PAs that I worked with were extremely competitive and functioned at a very high level both in the operating room and in the ER. These were essentially alpha PAs, and most had been in Orthopedics for several years. Being surrounded by very capable and confident PAs exposed me to their collective experience of both academic and real-world Orthopedic knowledge, which very quickly escalated my skills and knowledge base.

I would say probably within 2-3 months of being in that position, I had seen and dealt with more broken bones and acute patient issues than I had experienced being in my previous position for over 9 months. Of course, the increased acuity and patient volume helped to diversify my experiences, but I credit most of my foundational Orthopedic education to the PAs that were on the team with me at that time, as I absorbed their Orthopedic wisdom day in and day out. This was certainly not unique to just Orthopedics. We were friendly with other predominantly PA-run services, such as Medicine and the Medical ICU, and although those teams were smaller, they functioned in a very similar capacity with a clear seniority and mentorship program for new grads, which was closely aligned with the attending Physician leadership.

Now even though I felt supported at that job, I can say unequivocally, hands-down, that it was the most challenging professional experience of my life. The learning curve was extremely steep, and the other PAs on the team had pretty high expectations of my performance. God help you during x-ray review if your reduction was not absolutely perfect, or if there was some disagreement in your fracture management plan... they were ruthless and relentless, but because of their high expectations, I became much stronger, much better, much faster. To this day, there isn't anything in terms of acute Orthopedic Trauma that would terrify me. Open book pelvis? Bayonet femur deformity? I've had the pleasure of dealing with so many different situations because of my exposure, I'm able to remain calm and sensible now with most things that show up in front of me. I credit my comfort level 100% to the experiences I gained working at a large teaching facility being on staff with a larger predominantly PA team, with a strong mentorship program closely aligned with Physician leadership. As a new grad, that's what you want.

You might not like it, you might not even like me saying it, but a team like I described above is exactly what you need. You see, if you take my advice, and you fill in all the gaps of your education early on in your professional career by doing what's hard and uncomfortable, the remainder of your career should be relatively peaceful, and you can remain confident moving forward with your hard-earned real-world medical knowledge. As we said previously, the more skills and experience you have under your belt, the more cash you can command. Again, skills get you paid, period. This is definitely not the easiest way to get going as a PA, but it will be the most beneficial long-term. Remember my anesthesia friend from before? Please resist the urge to take the cushy job out of school where you are not challenged professionally or academically, I assure you, it will only hurt in the long run. Take the hard job upfront, put your time in, and in short order your sweat equity will turn you into the PA hero you were destined to become!

3

ALL THE OTHER PEOPLE

One of the things that can certainly be awkward when you graduate school and start looking for a job is this nagging feeling you just can't seem to shake...am I prepared for this? The answer is no, obviously not! You are very much not prepared! Now don't get me wrong, your program and education gave you the tools you need to enter the world of medicine. Essentially, they gave you the key to unlocking a door. Now the fun really begins, and you have to walk through it. As this is truly a journey, learning should not and can't stop once you graduate. Not only because you won't know what you're doing otherwise, but also because reputation is extremely important in medicine as we discussed.

In the real world of medicine, reputation is what will drive patients to your door, reputation is what will increase your salary potential, and reputation is what will dictate whether staff will be helpful or nonexistent when you need them the most! I can't tell you how many times I was in a fix on the floor, seemed like it was always 3 am. Thank God I had a reputation of being a good PA, and someone who took good care of their patients because the Nurses always bailed me out when I was in trouble. And if you think that's coincidental... guess again. By now I'm sure you realize that healthcare life can be smooth or full of friction depending on how you treat other people. Even if you decide to work outpatient office, you will have support staff, and if you want them to make your life easy, you have to treat people right! They have to know that you work hard! They have to know that you're in it with them, that it's not all about you!

So many times I have seen PAs graduate school, and all of a sudden become larger than life in their own minds. Without fail, 100% of the time, all the other people in healthcare will sniff right through that nonsense. The higher you promote your own personal interest over everybody else's, the lower you'll be seen, and that is not a very easy position to work from regularly. If you want longevity in this career, learn to treat other people with a mutual sense of respect. And not just other PAs, everybody. We are all on equal footing here, whether you are cleaning the floors, working in the cafeteria, at the bedside, or answering the phones...one team, period.

I sincerely believe one's capacity to thrive and succeed in their chosen profession is proportion-ately related to their ability to relate to others and treat them with a mutual sense of respect. So if they need help from you, help them! When I was working on the floors, I was never too busy to help someone change a dressing, even when it wasn't my patient! I was just doing the right thing and helping people when they needed help. If you maintain a similar kind of attitude and lead with service, I can virtually assure you that you'll have success in any chosen field of medicine.

Avoiding the embarrassment that gets so many PAs in trouble after graduation is predicated upon the idea that you now know what there is to know and you're too good to do certain tasks. If you sincerely believe that, you will be embarrassed regularly

because that is how the healthcare hierarchy inter-
acts with those who see themselves in that self-right-
eous light. The key? Again, remain humble! People
are getting sick, people are dying, people are having
tragedy in their lives...nobody gives a flying care that
you scored an 87 one time on a Renal exam in PA
school. Or that your new salary has upgraded you to
a brand new Cherry Red BMW 330 that you just
leased for way too much money a month. Leave that
nonsense out of work, away from patient care, and
have those conversations with your friends and
family.

Remember what we discussed earlier, patients are
making themselves vulnerable to you, and if you
dishonor that, you won't have a very long career in
medicine. In the same vein, you will likely be
spending a lot of time with the people you work
with, especially in a hospital setting, where hours
can be long, and tempers short. Treat not only the
patients but the people you work with daily with the
same level of dignity and respect you want to be
treated. We are all just trying to get through our day,
we just want to get back home to our pets or family
or whatever. It's not complicated, don't make it so.

Now then, how does everyone else in the healthcare world see you?

One of the things that bothered me the most when I first started in practice as a PA was that many other healthcare professionals didn't really know what to make of me. I would have oddly confrontational disagreements with a Physical Therapist, or get a questioning raised eyebrow by a seasoned floor Nurse over a treatment option I suggested for our mutual patient. I realize now that this is partly a personal issue in that I am somewhat of an introvert. The other part of this is that I am practicing in a role that is still not 100% widely understood. Personally speaking, there have been plenty of times where ambiguity arose as to the direction of treatment for a particular patient or with a treatment plan simply because the letters after my name were PA-C. You can imagine how frustration can easily build when people second-guess and question your treatment plans because of your title, and not because of your knowledge base. Indeed, you will face the same hurdles in practice as well, but hopefully a lot less than I did when I first started practice.

One of the ways you can start to combat some of this is to be first. The first to look someone in the eye, the first to smile, the first to put out your hand for a hand-shake, the first to say hello. Essentially, be confident enough to be the first to introduce yourself, even if you have to walk up to a wall of Attending Physicians during grand rounds. If you lead the conversation in this manner, you instantly disarm the other party and welcome more positive interaction. It's human nature to be on the defensive when we first meet someone new, so don't be in a position of reactivity, be in a position of proactivity. Take charge, not in a cavalier manner, but with subdued confidence aimed at expressing the fact that you are a professional, and expect to be treated as one. In-kind, you will treat the other party professionally. Guess what? It usually works. Sometimes, it won't. Why? Because people are people. We are human beings, and every single human being you know at some point in time is going to let you down. I am not perfect, so I do not expect anyone else to be perfect either, especially patients.

Much of what follows then has been learned the hard way over the past 10 years, but hopefully, my assessment on some healthcare players is at least somewhat helpful to you as you venture forth in your new profession. We have stuck primarily to the clinical side of things, and to the folks you may run into while going about clinical life. For the sake of completeness, however, we also wish to thank all of our colleagues in Administration, HR, Payroll, and all related departments for their daily contribution to the team!

ANCILLARY STAFF

Who are these folks? Of course, the people that provide the necessary support for things to keep running. These are the people that work in the cafeteria, environmental services, security, maintenance, engineering, and so forth. They typically will see you wearing a white lab coat and seeing patients, and assume you are a Doctor. In fact, they may refer to you as a Doctor. I got a kick out of this when I first graduated, made me feel important. Over time though, I grew to dislike it more and more, because it just meant that those people did not truly understand what it was that I did. These folks are the glue and the grease of the healthcare industry. Please treat them kindly. You couldn't do what you do if they didn't do what they do.

When I was in training I was instructed to correct people who mistakenly referred to me as a Doctor, I was supposed to let them know that I was a PA. While this sounds like a reasonable thing in theory, in practicality, it embarrasses people when you correct them. And frankly, as I said, I'm not sure some non-clinical people are even aware there is a difference. Correct them if you wish, just be kind about it.

NURSING ASSISTANTS

Many PAs I know utilized roles like that of a Nursing Assistant as the healthcare experience necessary to be a strong PA school applicant. CNAs, PCAs, NAs... you may see all of these different acronyms depending on where you live and work, but they all refer back to the same thing, Nursing Assistants. I did that work for many years before PA school...let me tell you, it is underpaid and overworked labor. Most of these folks have no choice but to work hard, as they have Nurses breathing down their necks. Almost universally, the Nursing Assistants I met along the way as a PA have been more than helpful to me, and typically have gone out of their way to lend me a hand when I needed it. These are solid folks, and you will often need their help to get something done.

If you end up working at a hospital, make sure you quickly identify who your "go-to" Nursing Assistants are on each floor you visit. You can usually pick out the hard-working ones because they are typically on the go, and moving rapidly. Their uniforms are tidy and crisp, and they take great pride in what they do. Those folks are an invaluable resource on the floors, especially because the Nurses are typically off doing

Nurse things and at times are hard to find. I can say that because my wife's a Nurse, so it's cool. This holds true if you are working an office-based job as well. Typically, medical offices employ Nursing or Medical Assistants, so try to align yourself with those that appear well put together and hard-working. Learning to work well with these folks can make or break your daily career life!

CLINICAL PROFESSIONALS

During rotations, especially in the hospital setting, you no doubt had to interact with a variety of different healthcare professionals that may have helped you deliver treatment. These folks didn't necessarily have as much direct patient involvement as say a PA, Nursing, or an attending Physician would have, but they are still an extremely important part of the overall team. Who are these folks? Think Respiratory Therapists, Physical Therapists and their Assistants, Nutrition, X-ray Technologists, and Pharmacists, just to mention a few. These are all additional players on that giant team that we have mentioned so often.

Now you likely won't be interacting with *all* of these folks *all* of the time, especially if you are working outpatient office, but the point is you have to be aware of them and understand that they are professionals too. In my career, I have found the vast majority of these professionals to be very open to communicating with PAs, and have generally been very helpful and supportive. They are typically very knowledgeable about their crafts. For example, when rotating through the ICU, I suspect you couldn't even pretend to understand the complexity of vent settings that the Respiratory Therapist was dealing with. So even though your credentialing may allow you to practice medicine and give you a significantly higher level of responsibility in comparison to say a Respiratory Therapist, it doesn't mean that your knowledge of their area of practice will supersede theirs.

Oftentimes, especially out of school, I had no idea what these folks were doing with the patients, and so I felt somewhat uncomfortable around them. I found this happening most often around Physical Therapy because we work so closely with them in Orthopedics. They would assess the patient and come describe their treatment plan to me, and I would typically have a glazed look in my eye because I didn't understand what it was that they did.

I found this to be true of so many other healthcare professionals, that I started to wonder what was wrong with me. Why didn't I know as much as they did? Short answer? Because I wasn't supposed to! I didn't go to Respiratory Therapy school, I didn't go to Physical Therapy school, and I didn't go to school to become a Pharmacist. I became a PA! This is why I strongly encourage you all to remain humble, especially in your first year.

I bring these folks up because I have found them to be an excellent repository of clinical knowledge and data that you can subsequently incorporate into your practice. As I started to interact more and more with these professionals, I simply asked them questions all the time. I stopped worrying that they would see me as incompetent if I didn't know exactly what they were doing. When you are genuinely curious about what another professional is doing, and ask good questions with serious intent, most of the time these professionals will be happy to share their knowledge with you.

It's not often these folks get very much credit for what it is they do day in and day out, and it feels good when someone takes a moment out of their day to talk with them about it. You'll be surprised how many little nuggets of gold you'll pick up from them which will make your clinical practice that much stronger! Learn to lean on these folks for information, don't be embarrassed to tell them you don't understand what it is that they're doing. Again come from that place of service and show them you seek to understand. They will respect you tremendously for it, and you will continue to develop that reputation as a rockstar PA.

NURSING

Ahhh yes...the Nurses. It doesn't matter what facet of healthcare you will eventually involve yourself with, you will most likely have to work with and alongside Nurses. The following commentary on Nursing has certainly changed over the years for me. I'm not sure why, but when I first graduated from PA school, I immediately developed an adversarial relationship with the Nurses. This is most likely because I was not comfortable nor confident in my role at that time. It can be somewhat alarming when during rounds a seasoned Nurse with 25 years of MedSurg experience has a better treatment option or suggestion than you do, a brand-spanking new PA.

Having essentially grown up professionally alongside Nurses, I have endeavored to better understand the Nursing profession and the interactions that we have daily while caring for patients. First and foremost, Nurses are our friends and allies in the day-to-day struggle of patient care. Their jobs are not easy, and neither is our job. Let me give you an example of a very personal experience to essentially illustrate the relationship that a healthcare provider and Nursing may have when ego takes charge....

As I mentioned earlier, in my second job out of PA school I was hired by a large inner city hospital system to join a large team of PAs and several Orthopedic Surgery residents. Again, this was a very challenging position at that time in my professional career. Not only did I not have significant knowledge of Orthopedic Trauma, the hours and call were grueling. This was a real deal Orthopedic Trauma position, with busy overnight call, and it scared the heck out of me as a junior PA. I made a lot of mistakes, however, I can look back now and say that it was all of that intense patient care, the acute trauma management, and stressful situations that made me much stronger over the years.

I distinctly remember going to work every day back then with a pit in my belly, knowing that at some point in time that day I would have to be performing something I wasn't sure I knew how to do, like any variety of fracture management, dislocation reduction, some surgical procedure, etc. There was a high degree of technical skill required on my part just to perform the nuts and bolts of the job. In addition, there was the actual patient management up on the floors, including the medical management of the patients who were admitted to the Orthopedic service. This is usually where my medical colleagues would laugh at me, because in Orthopedics we focus so much on musculoskeletal and mechanical injury, sometimes the more important medical stuff gets left behind.

Case in point, there was a post-surgical total hip patient that got to the floor one particular night I was on call. This patient had a bilateral hip replacement and did relatively well in the PACU before being transitioned to the floor. They did receive a spinal for anesthesia. Well, once up on the floor, shortly before midnight the patient started to develop progressive episodes of hypotension. The Nurse who was covering that patient on the floor was a well-seasoned MedSurg Nurse, who I had a significant amount of respect for. I happened to be on call that night with another PA who was very well-seasoned. Not wanting to look like a total newbie, I reassured this other PA on call with me that I would hold the fort, and that they could head to the call room for a few minutes of rest before the next trauma came in.

Well, probably every 30 minutes or so this Nurse would page me to come and assess the patient, she was concerned that the patient's blood pressure kept dropping. I became so entangled in other things on different floors, as well as other things going on in the ER that the significance of the dropping blood pressure did not weigh heavily on me, even though now as I write these words I can think how dangerous at that time it was. Every time that she would page me, I would simply ask her to bolus the patient with fluids, leave the patient supine, and monitor for care.

I could tell that she was becoming increasingly dissatisfied with my treatment plan because it wasn't working. I would tell her to bolus the patient, and pressures would continue to go down. This is not to say I did not go to assess the patient, I certainly did, but the point is I did not have the acute knowledge then to elevate that patient's level of care. The Nurse knew what needed to happen, the patient needed to go to ICU, for further workup and monitoring, as he was quickly exceeding the capacity of the floor to care for him. She suggested several times over several hours that the patient be upgraded to ICU for monitoring.

From what I can recall, there were no other signs of bleeding or hemorrhage, but the patient was becoming increasingly bradycardic without diffi-culty in breathing. His pain level wasn't changing, his blood pressure just kept getting lower and lower. Ultimately, the patient's systolic pressures dipped into the 60s, and it was about this point in time that my call partner rejoined me. When I told him what was going on with that patient, he became startled. He advised that I never sit on that kind of informa-tion and that the patient's level of care should be escalated immediately to ICU. Within 30 minutes, we had the patient transferred off the floor and to the ICU for evaluation and further monitoring care.

The patient ultimately did fine but required more intense medical treatment than I knew how to provide at the time. After the transfer, I met up with the Nurse and had difficulty looking her in the eye, because in her assessment, the patient should have been transferred out hours ago, and I played a dangerous game of overconfidence and under abil-ity. Although I did not verbalize it, I humbly accepted the fact that I was being cavalier with this patient's care, and I should have listened to Nursing advice hours earlier because it could've cost this patient their life. (Jennifer - if you are out there, you were right that night, and I should have listened to you sooner!) Thank God that things turned out the best for the patient and in the end, my relationship with that particular Nurse became even stronger.

This is just one in a series of many, many situations where as a new PA I did not have enough fundamental knowledge to put different pieces together so that I could make my way through acute challenges. The point is, I felt at that time superior to her because of a title I had worked very hard to obtain, and it unsettled me that she might know more than me at that moment. My ignorance could've been quite costly.

Shortly after that (and after many other similar experiences), I learned to stop seeing Nursing staff as adversarial but instead became much more collaborative with them. Do you know what? Sometimes they did have great suggestions on patient care. Sometimes they did have a better treatment option than I did at the time. For the Nurses that I became close with, it became more of a team than anything else, and I really enjoyed the feeling of working together with them in that capacity.

Now, this is not to say I did not still have poor interactions with some Nurses. I absolutely did. The fact that I saw Nursing as a collaboration in care did not change the fact that some Nurses did not share that same view. Some of them felt threatened by the Physician-PA relationship, and that insecurity can sometimes breed animosity towards PAs. You see, the Nursing profession has been around for a very long time, like the turn of the century-long. I'm sure everyone has learned of Florence Nightingale, the first Nurse. Nurses were historically assistants for Physicians in the early days of medicine. That dynamic has changed over the years, as Nurses have essentially gone from being drawn to the bedside to now being drawn to the PC, trying to keep up with all the electronic charting they are obligated to perform now.

As I mentioned earlier, my wife is a Nurse, and the level of charting she has had to accept responsibility for has increased dramatically over the last five years alone. This is why I mentioned earlier that you should rely on the Nursing or Medical Assistants on the floor to help move the day along more smoothly, the Nurses just simply can't keep up with all the charting. That being said, in my experience, Nurses who have come into practice more recently are much more open to the Physician-PA relationship, they are not threatened by it, and, enjoy that collaboration because they can more easily get a hold of you to discuss issues than they can the Physician, and it's often much less intimidating for them.

So, in essence, don't be an idiot like me and see Nurses as an obstacle. They are working on the same side of the patient as you are, and we are all just trying to get through our day. Don't make things adversarial and see them as a threat to you or the PA profession, you have your road to walk during the day, and so do they. They are professionals, so please respect what they do, even if at times there may be friction with how they interpret or assess your treatment plans. They are trained in the Nursing model, which is a very different way to develop care plans as opposed to the medical model. Either way, they want what you want, the best thing for the patient.

As long as you can remind yourself of this during the occasional heated exchange with Nursing, the more quickly you can diffuse the situation and get back on with your day. This will be much easier for younger Nurses, as opposed to the older Nurses who have admittedly seen a very dramatic change in their career. The entire medical landscape has changed significantly even over the last 10 years, just imagine what practice was like 25 or 30 years ago for some of these folks, and how challenging it is just to show up these days for work with all the modern intricacies. So please, be good to the Nurses, and most often, they will be good to you in return.

NURSE PRACTITIONERS

Up until now, I haven't said a word about Nurse Practitioners...but it's time. You all know and understand that Nurse Practitioners are out there and you'll have to engage them at some point in time during your career. Yes, technically they are competing for the same jobs as you are. You may even have received a significant bit of information on NP training versus PA training, especially as it relates to their clinical education. We will go more into depth about this shortly. The point here is *not* to create more friction between PAs and NPs, it's to make sure you have a basic understanding and foundation of NP education so that when you do encounter or have an exchange with an NP and you are at odds with either a medical or professional issue, you can fall back on what you know about NP education so that you can remain neutral and objective.

There has seemingly been a significant push, especially over the last several years, for NP programs to move towards a Ph.D. level of education. I am at risk of isolating myself here, but frankly, I feel that's ridiculous. If the profession as a whole wants to move towards a Ph.D. level education so that they can be Doctor Nurses, perhaps they should've gone to medical school in the first place. My thoughts on PAs and NPs obtaining a Ph.D. is that it should be strictly for academic or personal progression. If you wish to obtain a Ph.D. because you believe it will help further your personal achievements in some capacity, by all means, I 100% support that. But to assert a standard across all programs to move towards this level of education will only cause even greater separation between the Physician and Nurse Practitioner relationship in my opinion.

As it is, over my clinical years I have found that the Physician-NP relationship in some circumstances can be strained, because of the independence NPs tend to profess and assert. Indeed, in some states throughout the nation, it is perfectly acceptable for a medical practice to be individually owned and operated solely by an NP, and not have any significant Physician ownership or oversight. Instead, it has been my experience that the PA profession has attempted to more closely and further align itself with our Physician leadership, which is the way it should be! That relationship is foundational to our ability to practice medicine, and it should be respected as such.

Interpret that how you wish, but please understand that the Nursing profession has held powerful lobbying positions throughout the government for decades, as that profession is quite old. This is in stark contrast to the PA profession, which has not had the same opportunity over time to develop these relationships and governmental ties. This appears to be changing now, as we continue to step forward into further advocacy for our profession, especially at the legislative level. If politics by some chance interests you, you should consider using your voice or volunteering for local and more national PA advocacy groups, it not only helps the PA profession but all of healthcare as well.

So, to put it bluntly, and to not beat around the bush, you may have friction on occasion with NPs. Hopefully, this won't be the case on a regular basis, but I live in the real world and so do you (hopefully). I certainly have had my run-ins over the years, but for the most part, those exchanges were handled amicably, and professionally. But please understand that some NPs are going to see you as a threat to not only their jobs in healthcare but also as a growing organization on the healthcare landscape.

This comes back full circle to what I was mentioning earlier about respecting the Nursing profession, especially as a new PA. When you are insecure with your skills and abilities, as well as your knowledge base, you will easily feel threatened and have fear. So please, don't be fearful, become confident in your role, but remain humble in the practice of medicine and you will have more positive interactions than you'll know what to do with. Your career will subsequently be extremely rewarding. Start to see everybody as a boulder in your path, and your career will be lousy. Your choice my friend.

So if you haven't been given at least an introduction to NP education during your PA school training, you may find the following helpful. This is not an exhaustive examination of NP education, so if you would like additional information please look further into the NP programs themselves. Again we have included it here just so that you have a baseline level of understanding of their education versus ours, and how that sometimes can create a point of friction between the two professions.

NPs enter Nurse Practitioner programs with a certain baseline level of clinical experience required. Some go through Nursing school and become a

Nurse just so that they can go on and become a Nurse Practitioner. This may be the path of least resistance for some folks to practice medicine at a higher level than they otherwise could by not having to worry about going through formal medical school and subsequently residency. Nurse Practitioner programs are numerous throughout the country, and once accepted into an NP program, they choose a specialty area such as Family Practice or Pediatrics to focus on. It's important to understand they receive a focused education on their chosen specialty, needing to complete about 500 instructional hours and 500 clinical hours. The requirements are greater for DNP (Doctor Nurse) programs. PAs on the other hand are trained more in a generalist style similar to Physicians and need to complete about 1000 instructional hours and more than 2000 clinical hours. If you subsequently assess PA and NP education side-by-side, you can quickly see that there is a significant difference, with the PA education being much more strenuous and exhaustive.

NPs will be quick to point out that clinical education is not as important because they typically arrive at Nurse Practitioner programs with a certain amount of built-in healthcare experience. This is fine, and duly noted, but they cannot contest the fact that their training is 1/3 that of a PA. Therefore, fresh out of school, there is no comparison between a PA and an NP, in terms of baseline medical knowledge. Having said all that, about 4 to 5 years after graduation, most PAs and NPs will have amassed enough knowledge base and skill set to function in very similar capacities. So, it does even out. Please don't embarrass yourself and be quick to challenge NPs on treatment protocols and plans. Again, these are professionals too. They may be competing for your work, but I'm a big fan of mutual respect in the very multidisciplinary landscape called healthcare. If we don't play well with one another in the sandbox, nobody has any fun. Always remember to be elevating your profession, nobody can do it for you. When you act like a jerk, we all look like jerks.

PHYSICIANS

And now ladies and gentlemen, it's time to have a conversation about the elephant in the room...the Physicians! Well, let's just say it was a very steep learning curve when I first entered the PA profession. Dealing with Physicians and their specific needs daily can be exhausting, stressful, unpredictable, and at times humiliating. However, on the whole, I can't impress upon you enough how important these relationships have been for my life and my family's life.

I'll get to that shortly, but before entering a PA program, as I said before I was working in healthcare for many years. Physicians were always seen in my eyes as untouchable, you didn't look at a Physician, or talk to a Physician because they were too busy and too important to be bothered. I remember many times specifically as a Nursing Assistant when I was so nervous to give some information to one of the Physicians, that I nearly threw up from the intimidation! Ridiculous now, looking back on all that...but I was young and fearful. Things got a little bit better when I was working in the ER, because I had more direct patient information to exchange with the Physicians, and they more directly relied on the ER Techs for the usual scut work. But it wasn't until I started my practice as a PA that I came to understand that the Physician and PA relationship is wonderfully wholesome and synergistic in the right environment.

At first, I just didn't want to come across as a total idiot to the Physicians, and I'm sure we can all relate. When I was still new in my PA role, I was just as fearful and intimidated dealing with the patients daily as I was with the Physicians! This became more intense when I was questioned about treatment options or plans by Physician leadership, and understandably it took quite some time for that to subside. It will likely take some time for you as well, and that's very normal.

It got much easier for me over time as I developed experience and also began to accept the notion that I was providing a service for that Physician-PA relationship. Sometimes that service meant assisting in the OR, sometimes it meant helping with charting, sometimes it meant seeing a difficult patient instead of them as a human shield... whatever the case was, I was a service provider. When I remembered to frame my day-to-day tasks in this context as a service provider, it made dealing with criticism and questions a lot easier for me. In my mind, part of my service was to obtain and receive feedback, so that my service could improve in the future. Once I absorbed this, my professional life became much more peaceful as it related to the Physicians because I learned to separate my emotions from the criticism and accept their input as part of my daily service. Eventually, the criticisms become fewer and farther apart, as I learned to make better and better decisions, and that's when the PA-Physician relationship becomes really special.

Now, there are good and bad in all kinds, including Physicians. Some Physicians are going to be coming across to you as very pro-PA, and other ones as very anti-PA. Most Physicians I have found over the years to be somewhere in between. When we mentioned searching for an employment opportunity earlier, one of the things that we discussed was Physician oversight and collaboration. What I didn't mention at the time was that if you do not find an employment opportunity with the right kind of Physician leadership, then your job will likely totally suck. In fact, you may hate it. Why? Because good Physician leadership provides solid mentoring. And when you are new to medicine, and growing up in medicine, you need mentoring. Not just from other PAs, but from Physicians as well.

Physicians go through this process as well, in a much more structured format called residency. Yes, they are learning additional skills and knowledge to help care for patients during residency, but if you speak with residents, you will begin to learn they are also taught a variety of other things: local medical politics, the economics of medical practice, forming relationships and affiliations with other healthcare providers and institutions, and so forth. And that is just scratching the surface. They are given a whole set of educational lectures that have nothing to do with direct patient care, but everything to do with being a consummate professional and Physician. We do get a taste of this in PA school, but nothing like Physicians get.

This is why I am a big fan of aligning yourself with the right kind of Physician leadership especially right out of school, because the mentoring you would receive from these kinds of folks is priceless, and will take you much further in your career much faster. However, you have to be willing to accept mentorship, which always comes along with it the appropriate level of criticism. That's how we get better, we make adjustments to our behavior and medical practice based on recommendations from people who have done it before, done it for longer, or who can do it better than we can. Additionally, the right Physician leadership will have networking opportunities for you in the future, opportunities that may prove to be quite lucrative as your career progresses, provided you put in the time, energy, and effort required to be successful in what you want to accomplish. I'm a firm believer that as the PA profession continues to grow, so do our opportunities for expanding our reach in the healthcare landscape. I believe a big factor in this has been with PAs who have closely aligned themselves with progressive and open-minded Physician leadership with the right affiliations, unlocking the right doors at the right time.

I know what you're thinking...all Physicians are egomaniacs and self-centered, why would they want to help you get mentored? Let's explain because I assure you not all Physicians are egomaniacs and self-centered, although some of them certainly are and I've had the displeasure of working with many over the years! There are some qualities that you should be looking for that will help make this process easier for you. The key is to view your relationship with Physicians that's not one of benefit to you, but one of benefit to the Physician practice as a whole. You see, putting yourself in that position of being a service provider helps you see how Physicians look at PAs. I know this will offend some people, but like it or not, medicine is a business. A business, people! We are in the business of helping to care for others. Most places PAs will be working are businesses, and many will be for profit! This means that when these job opportunities become available, you are not being hired so the business can lose money. You're being hired so that you could help the business make money! When a Physician or organization decides to hire a PA, the idea is for that PA to help provide both tangible and intangible services which can be subsequently monetized. "Elio, what are you talking about now? Tangi-what?"

Well, an example of a tangible service is when a PA can see 20 additional patients alongside the Physician in the office per day and help increase additional patient flow and billing. Optimistically, billing and receiving revenue more than the cost of paying the PA is a win-win for the practice! Other tangible services would be as a first assist in the operating room, which can be billed for and helping to generate additional revenue for the practice.

An intangible service would be what I consider to be of convenience to the Physician. This can run the gamut, but an example would be when that difficult patient calls the office demanding to speak to the Physician who is standing next to you, but you take the call indicating that the Physician is off doing Physician things and is unavailable until next week, thus diffusing the situation and providing a remedy for your Physician. That's not something that can be billed or monetized but provides a service to the Physician and the practice. Another more mundane example would be if you are having a potentially slow day, and have spare time on your hands, you may help the Physician you work with see their patients more quickly, and more efficiently. Again not something you can usually directly bill for, but it does improve the ability of the practice to run efficiently and generate revenue.

While the tangibles are services that can be directly credited back to a PA in their line of service and probably make up the bulk of your daily obligations, the intangibles are the magic that provides the foundation of service. The intangibles facilitate patient flow in a less direct and immeasurable way, although I would argue they are more important than that which is measurable! I can't tell you what intangible services may mean for you in your future career, but you will know when you're doing them if it makes your Physician or groups life easier. Pro Tip - once you learn how to master the intangibles, Physicians will be unable to live without you! So while we are all interested in making money and being productive, coming from a place of service to our Physicians ultimately benefits our patients, sometimes directly and sometimes indirectly. And usually, if the Physician or practice is running well and efficiently with your services, your compensation tends to come up as well. This is the basis for things like bonus structures and incentives, which can make being a PA very lucrative in the long run. Just saying.

So who are these unicorns that we speak of that will essentially take you under their wing and teach you everything they know? Maybe they even help you make money and hook you up with some connections down the road to make even more money! Well, let's talk about it.

In my professional experience, this is not going to be typical of the older or previous generation of Physicians. If the Physician or group is within 5 to 10 years of retirement, then the PA practice is still likely an anomaly to them, and they likely have a poor understanding of the profession and the capacities at which PAs function, and so likely will not have a high level of respect for what you do. Which means they may pay low wages and treat you poorly. We can lovingly call these folks, the dinosaurs. Sorry, I know that's rude, but it's the truth. The older generation of medicine just wants to keep doing what it's always done, feels threatened by these changes, especially by PAs, and in my experience is overly conservative with their medical politics which tends to be exclusive of anyone else.

Let's be honest, these folks have been in medicine for a long time, they have already made a lot of money, and they have no intention of doing anything differently for the last portion of their career. They are most likely on autopilot, and not open-minded to what you can offer them or their practice. This is not ageism! We are not excluding people simply who are older! We are just pointing out the fact that the PA profession is still relatively young, and older Physicians simply have not had the opportunity or experience with PAs. Some have and that has worked out great. If that happens to be you and your Physician, that's a blessing! However, when you're fresh out of school, the last thing you want to do is go to war with an old battle ax in medicine and be talked down to regularly because the dinosaur feels you're unqualified to practice medicine. Unfortunately, these people are out there, and unfortunately, you may have to interact with them. Sorry guys, just keeping it real.

Far better instead to find opportunities where there will be much greater reception for what you do and what you can offer to a practice. In my experience, you'll have a better probability of finding a more rewarding experience if you seek out Physicians who are within the last 5 to 10 years of completing their training. I say that because those Physicians who have more recently left training have likely had some recent exposure to PAs during residency or fellowship. They have had the opportunity to form opinions about the PA profession, and whether they would seek to employ one in the future. Additionally, these folks who have left training more recently I feel in my opinion are more open-minded in terms of the PA profession and how it can help improve their practice flow and efficiency. In other words, they can see how a PA can help them and their business generate more cash.

In more practical terms, once you consider the length of full medical training, we are looking to align ourselves with Physicians who are in their mid to late 30s, to mid to late 50s. In my opinion, this represents the greatest opportunity for PAs to grow professionally, as there is theoretically a greater willingness to accept PAs within the practice. This of course cannot be applied universally. I know of a surgeon in their late 40s who has been around PAs his entire medical career, has hired several for his office, and routinely professes his dislike for the profession as he believes PAs are underqualified and overpaid. Again, these folks are out there, and we do have to engage them.

This holds true if you're seeking opportunities with larger organizations as well. You can't control of course who the Physicians are that work in the practice, but you can certainly decide whether it would be a good fit or not. If the practice is comprised of several blowhard dinosaurs, you likely won't have a fantastic experience. However, if the practice is filled with a blend of less senior Physicians and preferably with additional PAs, that would be a much better fit, especially for a new grad.

Please understand all of this information is pretty much specifically for new grads. I say this because once you've been in practice for several years, you begin to grow confidence and know how to handle yourself in sometimes unfavorable Physician interactions. This can and will happen as you are questioned about your decision-making and treatment plans, especially by the lovely dinosaurs. However, when you have experience on your side, your confidence is dramatically higher, and you know how to stand up for yourself, your medical decision-making, and for your profession. So when more experienced PAs look for jobs, they're not necessarily looking for mentorship... they are looking for opportunities to make money and to continue doing what they love to do in the least abrasive way possible. When you're a new grad though, you don't have the luxury of experience. Again, you have to earn that in the trenches as we all do.

The other thing to watch out for when looking for jobs, is you actually want that Physician leadership to be present. I talk to so many new PAs who tell me they have great jobs because the Physicians are never around, and they get to do what they want. I understand why they say this, but it hurts my heart to hear that because I know they could be so much stronger in their medical practice if their Physician leadership was around and available to them.

In most instances of my medical career, I gained the most knowledge and developed the best skills when my Physician leadership was directly accessible to me during my day. Now, was this always the case? Of course not! You're often being paid to be around when the Physician can't be. For example, in my most recent job, I was in the office seeing patients while the Physician was in surgery. If I wasn't in the office seeing patients while they were operating, the Physician would lose productivity because they can't be in two places at once!

So at times, it's understood that you will be on your own as a PA. That's OK, you were given a basic skill set during PA school. However, in my experience to grow and thrive as a PA you need to dig in and utilize the exceptional resource that you have in your Physician leadership. Then, when you become a more experienced PA, the direct Physician supervision becomes much less important as you've already developed a wide base of knowledge and skills...

perhaps they just need to be available by text or email on occasion, as it was for me with my most recent job.

So, what I'm telling you is that your needs will change from the time that you are a new grad to that of a more experienced PA. You will crave Physician supervision initially, and you should! But you will likely be burdened by it as you develop experience in the field, and frankly, you may be severely annoyed when your Physician is around at that time in your career. The change happens for most PAs I think, and only you will know when it's time to make that adjustment in your career. The point is, it's not a static situation. Like all things, your comfort level and experience are dynamic and your needs from the Physician leadership will need to be adjusted to reflect that. Initially, however, you will need it!

PATIENTS

Yes folks, the reason we go to work every day, and try to be better versions of ourselves...the money, I mean the patients. Over the years I have laughed with, cried with, been angry with, been disappointed with, and probably shared too much with, the patients. They will test you, question you, admonish you, and at times humiliate you. They will also, however, respect you, admire you, trust you, and love you.

There's no question in my mind when I say that some of the most challenging experiences of my life have been at a patient bedside. There are moments in medicine where you can feel yourself growing while undergoing intense patient situations. I pray for all of you that every patient interaction you have will be positive and that the right outcome occurs for every patient. But this is life, and we all know that cannot be a reality. We all know that not every patient will do well, that not every patient wants to see a PA, and that not every patient will respect what you do. There are so many other patients that do though! I would say with 100% comfort, that it had become increasingly rare for me to encounter someone who did not want to see me in the office.

More often than not, patients preferred to have seen me versus my supervising Physician because I typically had a few extra minutes to spare, and that meant a lot to them.

When I first graduated from PA school, I was extremely sensitive toward patients that I knew did not want to see me, knowing that they wanted to only interact with the Physician. I took this very personally of course and felt threatened. I can look back now in my later years, and forgive myself for being so ridiculous. I understand now that my sense of self was tied quite strongly to this idea of being a PA, and that when someone challenged my idea of that self, my ego became bruised. I suppose it's because I worked so hard at becoming a PA, sacrificed so much to finally get into a PA program, and gave so much time, effort, and money just to be able to call myself a PA.

Without becoming too esoteric, we are not the titles after our last name. We are not just a summation of our education or experiences. We are human beings attempting to coexist with one another. When we latch onto or attach ourselves too tightly to labels and descriptions, we are at the mercy of other people utilizing these labels and descriptions in any way they choose...making us quite fragile. When people attempt to summarize your capabilities (or lack thereof) based on a few letters after your name, it can sometimes feel as if you are being summarized as well. So it's not Julie the PA who I don't want to see, it's Julie. And she happens to be a PA. Do you see the difference? As I said before, medicine is fickle. There is an old aristocracy in medicine, and although many of those paradigms have been shifting in the last decade or so, the aristocracy remains.

How do we deal with this overtly distasteful challenge to our profession and one that can raise its ugly head daily for the PA profession? My advice? Don't! You don't have to deal with any of that nonsense. As a reminder, you are a professional. You have worked extremely hard to be able to call yourself a PA, and have endured and sacrificed much to practice medicine. Nobody and I mean nobody, has the authority or the right to make you feel insignificant or a lesser-than based on your professional credentialing. Additionally, you do not have to prove this value to any other single person. The only one who must be 100% at peace with their professional and academic career is you!

So when that sort of ugly exchange occurs, and I guarantee you at some point in your professional career it will occur, and the patient indicates that they are not interested in seeing you but perhaps your supervising Physician, remain calm. Do not take it personally. Please remember that the way people treat you has nothing to do with you, and everything to do with them. If you feel as if the interaction will not be beneficial for the patient, then do not engage in it unless you have to.

When I was working in the office setting, if I saw a patient that felt strongly about seeing my supervising Physician, I would simply let them know that I could of course facilitate getting them on their schedule, but that would mean likely waiting an additional 6 to 8 weeks to receive care. Once they heard this, miraculously they felt inclined to accept my care. Why? Because at a baseline we are all a little selfish. We all want to feel that we are special, and deserve royal treatment. In essence, here in the States, we all feel a little entitled to our healthcare.

The fact that some patients consider any care other than that of a Physician to be sub-standard can be difficult to overcome. You can help educate them to alleviate some of that ignorance by demonstrating just how capable of a provider you are. But Hunny, you can't fix stupid! No matter how hard you try, some patients will not want anything to do with you. Best to find that out early in the relationship and move on, figuratively and professionally!

Now while we are on the subject of patients, I think we have to cover a certain controversial topic on the other end of the spectrum. We all live in the real world, real human beings, doing real stuff. There are real emotions at hand, and at times the professional and ethical lines become blurred. Many times over the years, I have observed or have become peripherally aware of colleagues who have become either romantically or physically involved with one of their patients.

This is a delicate topic, as the professional implications involved with violating the patient and provider relationship can be disastrous. Remember, this relationship is one based on trust and vulnerability. If you decide that pursuing a relationship with one of your patients is an appropriate thing to do, please make sure to immediately and definitively separate yourself from their care, as to have no further medical decision-making for them. It's the right thing to do. And while it may be wildly entertaining to find out which Physician or PA is having an affair with so-and-so, just remember how dysfunctional and disastrous those situations can be for everyone involved.

Unfortunately, I have witnessed many marriages and relationships fall apart in medicine due to illicit and controversial behavior with patients and other staff. Families have been shattered and torn apart...children separated from parents. Please don't be careless with your professional privileges and the power that comes along with them. And don't laugh, snicker, or jeer when you hear about that affair...come up higher, don't repeat the gossip, and keep your opinions to yourself. Light cuts through the darkness.

So we always want to be mindful and extremely responsible with our patient relationships, because the vast majority of the time those relationships can be very rewarding and extremely positive. If you're like me, when you graduated from PA school you likely took the Hippocratic Oath, and hopefully, you did not say the words just to say them. You took an oath and you meant it. You have to stand by the words that you've said, even when it becomes challenging.

Although you are the one with the education and training in medicine, I have found time and time again that it is indeed the patients that teach us. I have been exposed to so many different cultures, religions, theology, and spiritual practices, you name it! All of these different experiences have opened my eyes to all the different ways that we thrive as human beings.

One of the things I learned along the way with patients is this notion of medical skepticism. In my most recent job, I was practicing medicine in the southeast United States. A large percentage of my patient population happened to be African-American. Me being Caucasian, I had to learn that culturally there was a significant amount of medical skepticism from the African-American community in the area where I was practicing medicine. Because of this, when I sat down to interview patients, I had to be aware that I may not be receiving the full story, the full list of symptoms or complaints. It became much more detective work than usual with the community, at times significantly affecting my ability to diagnose appropriately because there was a legitimate reluctance to share information.

The bottom line is that for that patient population, there was limited trust given to medical providers. I had to adapt my style of interview and my questioning so that patients became much more comfortable with sharing information. If I wasn't successful with this, I would not be able to treat the patients as completely as I could, because I didn't overcome the gigantic initial hurdle of trust building. I know we mentioned this before, but the patients make themselves vulnerable to you, lots of times reluctantly so that you can care for them. If they don't let you in, you can't care for them. For them to let you in, there has to be a baseline level of trust. Although this seems overly simplistic, in the real world trying to see 100 patients or more a week, this becomes more challenging than it seems.

During your training, you likely heard or had some education on developing rapport with patients. Being able to quickly and efficiently develop a charismatic and meaningful relationship with a patient is foundational to your ability to practice medicine. If you can't develop rapport with a patient quickly and efficiently, you can't care for them to the best of your ability. That means that the patient might not get the care that they deserve, and the onus is on you to develop that skill.

Developing rapport is not the responsibility of the patient, they are not coming in to see you so that they can work on developing their rapport-building skills. This is all about you and developing as a professional in medicine. You will see that the highest-rated and best-liked providers in medicine typically are the ones that can develop the strongest and most genuine rapport with patients and their families. Now, this is not something that you're typically taught in school, it's a skill set you develop by dealing with people over time. Reading body language, facial cues, vocal tones... these are all things that come together to develop the basics of communication which again is primarily nonverbal. And guess what, you have to become an expert at it!

Things like developing clinical suspicion when you feel a patient may be drug seeking or you may be suspecting elder abuse... you need to develop these skills quickly after you graduate. There are a plethora of resources concerning nonverbal communication out there, not just books but free online courses, and even really great YouTube videos. I sincerely urge you to seek out these resources and become proficient in that skill set. I can't impress upon you enough on how much it will improve your medical practice, as well as your overall relationship-building throughout life. Master non-verbal communication!

LAWYERS

While this is not an exhaustive list of all the different kinds of people you interact with in the healthcare landscape, we did try to keep the list as concise and relevant as possible. Unfortunately, we probably couldn't have a relatively complete conversation about the different people you may deal with if we didn't discuss lawyers. You've probably already been given a warning or at least some sort of conversation, maybe even a lecture, regarding litigation in health-care. There is no way around it, healthcare is a very fertile ground for litigation. We are going to talk about my perspective and situations I've been in over the years that have given me pause and concern for the practice of medicine. While at times some of the commentary may seem disparaging against our friends in law, the conversation is merely meant to convey the very real and oftentimes painful burden of litigation as a result of your day-to-day life as a PA.

During my training, I do remember quite vividly receiving a lecture series about medical-legal issues, and how they pertain to the current state of health care as a whole. One of the things that stuck out at that time was when the professor indicated that it would not be a matter of if, but when, you were faced with a lawsuit during your profession in healthcare. At the time, that really scared the heck out of me. I had never been in any kind of legal trouble before, and the thought of being the subject of a lawsuit because of my job or going to work was quite alarming. However, once you get out there practicing medicine, you realize that the system is set up in many different ways at many different levels to decrease the probability of litigation.

For example, while working at a larger hospital system in one of my previous jobs, the other PAs and I would at times find ourselves chuckling at some of the Nursing notes. We found that the Nurses would at times practice defensive documentation when there was an issue with a patient, or documenting in a way that shifted responsibility from themselves to the person they had notified, namely one of us PAs. Professional finger-pointing, if you will. *Not it!* Turns out, when you get out there, you notice that a lot of what happens in medicine is this shift in liability as it pertains to the patient. In my very humble opinion, it is in this shift that people get into the most trouble. Let me explain....

Much of the day-to-day routine happenings in medicine involves an exchange of information. Sometimes this information is incredibly simple, like a temperature or a blood pressure reading, sometimes it's incredibly complex, like when Heme-Onc is consulted for your 27-year-old patient with unexplained weight loss and widespread petechiae. Once that information has been gifted to the next accepting party, that provider or group is now woven into the tapestry of that patient's care, forever. So as you go about your business of caring for people on a day-to-day basis, you begin to accept responsibility for their medical care, as well as your decision-making, all based on some information you receive. Because these exchanges in healthcare are so common, there are multiple opportunities for things to go wrong.

We all know the dangers of documenting incorrectly or performing a task or skill outside of our standard routine level of care. But the truth is, there are land mines of medical-legal issues waiting for you all over the healthcare landscape. Sometimes, you'll have no idea you've stepped on one. And if you're unfortunate enough to have stepped on a big one, it may lead to litigation. We can do a whole other book just on the medical-legal issues you may face daily as a PA. Frankly, that would be depressing, so we're not doing it. The reason we even bring up this topic is because I just want you guys to be hyperaware, from a real-world perspective of a person who has been practicing and been exposed to this over the years. If it doesn't eventually impact you directly, it will certainly impact someone you know.

Thankfully, I have never been succesfully sued, but I most certainly have been served papers, and I most certainly have been named in suits that were settled out of court. It is a very strange experience to have the County Sheriff walk into your office with a nice white envelope and official seal on it, indicating you are being deposed. Stranger still is after you wrap your head around what's happening, you realize you may have seen this patient only one time 3 years ago, and have absolutely no recollection of caring for them. Stranger yet is then sitting down across from 2 unsympathetic veteran lawyers who are eager to cut you down to size and have you admit wrongdoing during the course of your care for them. I don't want to get too much into the weeds with this, but just know that it's happening, and you must be careful.

I can probably guess with some certainty that you've already been spoken to about this during your training, but it bears repeating here...as we say in surgery, please measure twice and cut once. In other words, be mindful of what you are doing out there. You will not know exactly what to do with every situation. However if you lean on the appropriate resources, lean on your education, and use that funny thing called clinical judgment, you will do fine. Be careful with the information that you have been trusted with. Don't do what I have done in the past, and sat for hours on a post-surgical patient with tanking blood pressures on the floor, because I didn't know what to do. If that patient died, my career would have likely ended then. So, get help when you don't know, speak to somebody smarter than you, and don't jeopardize your license. Have a low threshold to bounce ideas and questions off other people, again this is a giant team effort and no one can have success in this by themselves.

If your intentions are good, and you always act within the boundaries of what you have been taught, you will most likely avoid really bad situations. Of course, if you are put in a situation where you need representation, please don't go with Uncle Larry's "guy", or one of the fly-by-night law offices you see advertised during a Jerry Springer commercial break. Do your homework, and talk to your attending Physician. Physicians are no strangers to lawsuits, they often have an excellent lawyer a phone call away, so use them!

4

HOW TO EARN MORE

O K... let's talk about everybody's favorite topic... money! OK OK, I know you probably didn't get into the PA profession strictly for the money, but I'm sure it was a pretty large topic of conversation when you were deciding. Let's be honest, PAs make really good money. A six-figure salary in 2022 can provide a great lifestyle in most parts of the country, and in others maybe not so great! In comparison to other parts of the world, however, any salary a PA can command is fantastic to what some people subside on.

So, you graduate school, you probably have some student loans, maybe even a little (or a lot) of a credit card situation, and you need to know how to get that cash flow going. I do know some PAs who have made a lot of money over the years...and you can too if you become proficient with your chosen skill set and market yourself appropriately. I can tell you that my personal best to date I made 250k in one year. That's what some Family Medicine Physicians are making guys. Now I was working my tail off that year, and it was a combination of my baseline salary, bonus incentives, and working some Urgent Care. But it does give you an idea of what's possible if you need to grind for a year or two to catch up on some debt. Sure, you may find positions in other parts of the country where you can make a heck of a lot more than that, but for my area in the Southeast US, that amount of money was fantastic for that year. How did I do it? Let's see....

I've already mentioned that my entire career has been in Orthopedic Surgery and its subspecialties. It turns out that in medicine when you have invested time to gain even a little bit of information, you can leverage that information (mixed with a little bit of hard work) and yield some pretty good results. In my particular case, I was working a salary position at a private Orthopedic office, so basically, weekdays were 8 to 5, with an OR day sprinkled in here and there as well.

This particular private office had an Urgent Care set up that was staffed outside of the normal business hours and paid a very attractive hourly rate to providers who would work it. Since Urgent Care was functional after hours, namely 5:30 pm to 9 pm, and open on the weekends, they paid a premium to entice people to work it. I would typically finish my normal schedule around 5 pm, so I could easily start the Urgent Care shift around 5:30 pm, and be wrapped up by 9 or 9:30 pm after charting. While not something I wanted to do forever, I did take advantage of this arrangement and one year worked roughly 12 to 15 of these Urgent Care shifts a month, which dramatically increased my income (and taxes!)

This concept is well-known in medicine, and it's called moonlighting. That's nothing but a fancy term people in medicine use when they are working a second job. Well, when you are early in your career, and you are eager to make money as well as increase your knowledge base, moonlighting can be a very good way to increase your earnings and expose your-self to additional avenues of medicine. There are several different combinations that you can attempt with this. For example, while working in my outpatient Orthopedic office, I had a PA colleague who was moonlighting in the local ER, picking up 12-hour shifts on Saturday or Sunday to help augment her income. She used this income to help quickly pay down student loan debt. Yes, it does mean working on a weekend sometimes. But the truth remains that if you are not willing to work hard, you will likely not get very far in life.

I did something similar when I was working in inpatient Orthopedic Trauma. Those days were much less predictable, and I was taking 24-hour overnight inpatient call. My typical schedule then was to be at work by 5:40 am, get sign out and assignments, head to the floors for rounding by 6 am, meet with the attending Physician for a case review at 7 am, and surgeries typically started by 7:30 am. I would normally operate all day Monday and all day Tuesday. However, on Tuesdays, instead of going home around 4:30 or 5 pm as I did on Mondays and Fridays, I stayed in-house until 7 am the following morning. The fun typically started around 5 pm as the traumas started rolling in and we were often hustling until 6 am the next morning.

Well after I came off-shift Wednesday morning, I would be post-call and pretty much worthless. Thursdays however, which were supposed to be my day off, I started moonlighting at an Outpatient Orthopedic office that was close to my home. I negotiated a per diem rate with a surgeon to help him see patients in his office and would work about 6 to 8 hours a week on those Thursdays. While I certainly wasn't killing it at this particular moonlighting spot, it was some very nice extra money that I certainly appreciated, and at that time really needed. With my salary position and schedule set up at the hospital, I was able to work for this extra money during the work week and continue to primarily have my weekends off which for me was the best of both worlds.

There are many different ways to structure moonlighting, but I found that the practice of moonlighting was much easier for me to facilitate while working in the hospital versus in the outpatient office. The reason for this was while working in the outpatient office, I was limited to moonlighting outside of business hours. Well, after a while, being away from family in the evenings and for chunks on the weekends tends to get old pretty quick. However, when I was working in the hospital, with my salary schedule, I had a whole day off during the week which I could use to moonlight during business hours, which is more attractive to those with families.

If you are not at a point in life where you have to worry about being home in the evening for family obligations, then picking up moonlighting shifts on weekends and evenings would likely be the most lucrative option for you. Again things like working Urgent Cares and shift work in the local ER can help bolster your income and get you into a much more stable financial position more quickly. This is not earth-shattering stuff guys, if you want to make more money, you have to work more. Moonlighting gives you that opportunity without having to pick up shifts at Pizza Hut.

If you think you may want to moonlight in the future, make sure this is on your radar when you are looking at job opportunities. Many employers are upfront about needing additional coverage by providers, and this may open up the door for you to moonlight more efficiently once you are up to speed. How soon that happens is up to you. I first dabbled in moonlighting after having been with a particular organization for six months. It was about this time that I felt comfortable enough with the systems, the other Physicians, and their protocols to moonlight with little Physician supervision. Again, this will come down to your comfort level and desired income.

Another way to increase your earning potential is of course to utilize the dreaded call. We could write an entire book on the topic of call, but we'll do our best to keep it brief here. Basically, the call comes down to a couple of different flavors... that which you get paid extra for, and that which you don't. Typically, it's not optional either, it's mandatory. More and more, as healthcare systems and provider offices attempt to trim the fat, they are incorporating a call structure into the baseline salary so that you are effectively required to take call but will not get paid extra for it.

My very first job as a PA was set up like this. The call at that time was not bad, it was 4 pm to midnight covering 2 different ERs, and after midnight the calls got routed to the Physicians. I did not get paid extra for working four to midnight, it was just included in my routine obligations once or twice a week.

Knowing what I know now, I would never sign up for a gig like that again. That's one of the great benefits of gaining experience in your role, is that you can negotiate call and salaries, especially when they are asking you to work outside of normal business hours.

For me, anytime outside normal business hours is premium time, which means you should be getting paid more during those hours, period. Premium hours include evening hours and weekend time and contrary to popular belief, premium time cannot be made up during normal business hours throughout the week. Therefore, it's very important that if you are required to work those hours you are compensated fairly for it.

Now, as a new grad, you will not have much ground to stand on for the sake of negotiation. This is the point in life where you may have to just take your medicine. However, after a year or so, and you have some good experience under your belt, these items become more negotiable. Subsequently, in jobs I worked after this first one I became wise to the whole call situation and compensation there off. I did not work any more jobs where the call was incorporated into the salary structure. Quite simply, if an employer is not willing to compensate me for my premium time, I will be looking elsewhere. I suggest that once you have some experience, you adopt this mindset as well.

A brief word of caution...please pace yourselves. It's very tempting once you know what you're doing and low-hanging fruit is available, for you to go picking. In healthcare, now more than ever, it's very important that you have a firm sense of balance in your life. The healthcare world is complex, fast-moving, emotional, high-stress, and unforgiving. You must have some good systems and resources in place to counterbalance a lot of the negativity you'll absorb day in and day out.

Please understand that you will be engaging with patients who will be trying to offload a significant amount of pain and suffering onto you daily. What you do with all of that accumulated pain and suffering is up to you, but the most healthy thing to do is to discharge it in some regular and healthy self-directed practice. Exercise, meditation, prayer, etc. In your first year in medicine, you probably won't have the time or the wherewithal to develop these practices, but after a year or so, you begin to understand that the patients can and will take a lot out of you.

Learn to relax, learn to take good vacations, learn to decompress, and forget about work when you're not there. So, even though you might need the money, please pace yourself and make time for the good things in life. You've earned that.

5

REAL LIFE MONEY

As I mentioned earlier, my family comes from humble beginnings. As the son of immigrant parents, I was the first one in my family to go to college. Higher education and the wealth oftentimes associated with it were not concepts that were available to me as I was growing up. What was ingrained in me was the classic notion of blue-collar hard work, and if you work hard enough, you can make some good money and have nice things in life.

So money wasn't exactly a dinnertime conversation in my house growing up. It was typically talked about after my siblings and I went to bed at night, and my parents would stay up to argue about bills or needing money for so and so. The conversation about finance and how to deal with it was taboo. My father did not trust the banks and preferred to keep his money in cigar boxes. Seriously. Because of this, when I grew up I did not have a really strong fundamental understanding of money, how to manage it, and especially how to make it work for me.

I was probably well into my 30s before I started to take finance more seriously, and I know it hurt me financially to start later in life than most people. So in the section that follows, I'll try to give you some real practical advice in regards to how to deal with the new cash flow from your new job. You may have grown up in a situation where you were given education and understanding about money at a young age. For everyone else like me, we had to learn on the fly. These are just my opinions, obviously not legitimate financial advice...if you need additional planning or information, please seek the services of a fiduciary financial planner, and preferably one who will not be looking to make money off products you buy from them.

Most new grads coming out of PA school will command a fairly decent salary, likely one that is much higher than anything they've ever received. The jump can be very impressive, and if you don't have good foundational money management in place, you can get into trouble quickly. It probably should go without saying, but you don't want to go ahead and start spending all of that money that is coming in on things like new cars and jewelry. While these things are certainly nice, and you are entitled to have nice things for working hard, also please understand that at the end of the day it doesn't matter how much money you make. What matters only is how much you keep. Managing your cash flow and expenses is part of becoming a professional, and having the skills in place so that you can make good decisions at the right time, will take you financially much farther.

So how do you begin to understand what to do with the money? Well, while this is not a book on money management, I can tell you some basic information that you can use as a starting point, and from there decide how to best manage your cash flow. You see, your financial life and wealth-building will occur over a lifetime. You won't just sit down and run the numbers one time and expect to be good for the next

40 years. You have to assess and reassess your finances and your wealth-building goals on a regular basis.

One of the most common budget formulas I see tossed around is the 50/20/30 Plan. What this plan basically says is that you take 50% of your income and allocate it towards housing and transportation. This includes things like gas, car insurance, and all the trappings associated with either owning a home or renting. 20% is then allocated towards wealth building, such as investments, 401(k), etc. The remaining 30% will be spent on discretionary expenses and wants, not necessarily needs. Although popular because of its simplicity, it can be disastrous as it almost suggests that you can spend up to 30% of your income on wants and be fine. While this may be true if you were further along in your financial life and had minimal debts and high income, this is not true of the new PA school grad. With NCCPA saying that the median student loan debt coming out of school is roughly 110k these days (and often much more!), spending 30% on wants with that kind of loan debt is simply irresponsible.

When I first started making money, I would read finance books and blogs, or listen to podcasts of different people giving financial advice, all in an attempt to make myself smarter with the money I was making. One of the people that made sense to me in the financial world was Dave Ramsey. You may have heard about him before, or even listened to his radio show on occasion, but basically, he makes finance and building wealth doable for the common person. Again, I was very financially illiterate. I stumbled around with my finances quite a bit, but I did see that the things Dave Ramsey was teaching and helping people with were easy concepts that I could follow. One of the things that Dave talks about is something called a Zero-Based budget. In comparison to the plan mentioned above, this way of budgeting has you account for every dollar. Although budgeting seems as exciting as watching paint dry, I assure you that watching cash pile up in your checking account is indeed thrilling. Remember, if you can track it, you can control it.

The plan essentially has you take your income and tease out all the expenses which we would call "needs". Think about things like food, utilities, housing, and transportation. This will likely be a pretty large chunk. After you separate all these needs, you then attempt to prioritize things with the remaining cash depending on where you are in life. Again, as a new grad, you will likely have some credit card debt and student loan debt. After you have paid the minimum on these, you can now take any additional remaining monies and either start building an emergency fund or attacking more of that debt. The bottom line is that at the end of the month, 100% of the income is being put to work for you.

The idea behind having every dollar being made accounted for is so that you are not tempted to spend hard-earned money on dumb things, at a time in your life when you don't need dumb things. Yes, yes, I know...you have worked hard and deserve nice things. Look, I'm not saying to not have nice things. I'm just saying that as a professional, you don't want to be the only person in the parking garage driving a busted-up banana yellow '87 Civic with crank windows because you can't manage your cash flow. (Not hating on the '87 Civic, by the way, those are classic cool.) So put in a little time to this once you start making some money, and don't overcomplicate it. The reason why I like this plan is because it's incredibly simple, and even I could follow it. For more information on this, do a Google search on Zero-Based

Budget, there are many resources available to help you get started!

Here is what that might look like in the real world. According to the most recent salary data I could find, the average PA is making 115k/yr. I know, some are making much more, some much less, but let's agree on 115k. For the sake of the example, let's take that 115k and immediately multiply that by 65%, and we get roughly 75k. Why 65%? Well, we have to make sure we pay out Uncle Sam and the remaining deductions on our pay stubs. If this is your first real job, welcome to the world of taxes! As part of your deductions on your paycheck, you will see taxes for Medicare, federal and state income tax, and Social Security tax, amongst others. Additionally, you will likely be provided a health insurance package provided by your employer, with shared expenses deducted from your pay. Also, if the company offers a retirement package, and you decide to participate in this (which you should) these monies will also be deducted at this time. So, even though you are now making over 6 figures, you'll be in a higher tax bracket and coughing up more dough to pay Uncle Sam. That 115k melts away really fast after taxes and deductions!

So back to that 75k. For the sake of simplicity, if you divide that by 12 months, we get around $6200 a month. Therefore, in our real-world example, if you get a job as a PA making the current median income of around 115k, your real-world dollars coming in after taxes and deductions is $6200 a month...not too shabby. But unless you're living in mom and dad's basement, you'll have to rent or buy a home.

A quick search on housing affordability will show you that 30% or less of your income should go towards housing. In our example, that would be around $1800 or less. Can you find a rental for this much money? Certainly, especially if you got a roommate. Can you get a mortgage these days in 2022 with this much money? Maybe, if you spend less than 350k on a home and put down 20%. Easy to do out of PA school? No, and in some parts of the country housing is extremely expensive. It took me years after I graduated from PA school to save up the money for a down payment on a home. During that time, I rented an apartment with my then girlfriend, splitting our living expenses. We eventually did it though, and of course, the end result was great because we bought a home! Add in the fact you need to pay utilities like electricity, gas, water, and internet (avg is $400/mo for me), and you are left with about $4000/mo ($6200-$1800-$400=$4000). Still not too shabby.

We need wheels. One of the first really stupid things I did after graduating from PA school was to go out and buy a brand new truck, costing me nearly $50,000. Payments on that truck were around $650/mo. I look back now and shake my head, but I know that some of you out there have a need and want to do those kinds of things. If I can talk you out of it, take it from my experience that there are better things to do with your money. However, if you must have that new car, go ahead and buy it. Understand though that you will always lose money on cars unless it's a collectible. Cars are mechanical things, and mechanical things eventually break down. They need to be maintained, and you have to of course factor in fuel charges and auto insurance as well.

A much smarter financial strategy is to buy a lightly used car (gasp!), that is 2 or 3 years old, where the initial owner has taken the majority of the depreciation hit on the vehicle. This way, you are getting a relatively newer car at a deep discount, you still look good in your new(er), and your wallet feels even better! Just think about it, that's all I'm trying to say.

If you can keep transportation costs to $500/mo or less (including gas, insurance, and payments/lease), you would be ahead of the game! After taking $500 from our remaining $4000, we are down to $3500/mo.

Unfortunately, most of us will have to finance our education. The burden of student loan debt in this country has become difficult to read about, it hurts me to see so many young people being saddled with tremendous debt loads right out of school. I also understand that you have to do what you have to do. I graduated from PA school with a mountain of student loan debt, and it remained a tremendous weight on my shoulders for a very long time. Most of you reading this will have to make student loan payments after you graduate, and I sympathize with you because I was there too.

There's a lot of variability in the data in regards to PA school student loan debt, the numbers are everywhere from 100k to 200k. For our example, I will use a figure of 120k, because it's a commonly referenced number. Loan payments for that size loan for a 15-year term and 6% interest are around $1000/mo. Once that is paid, we're down to $2500/mo. Add in a couple of credit card payments of $250/mo, we're now at $2000.

Oh yeah, we have to eat. The PA school diet of Ramen and Diet Pepsi should probably get an upgrade now that you have graduated. If you're buying fresh fruits, vegetables, and lean sources of protein, you should expect to pay roughly $100/week in groceries. Since you are a young professional, we know you want to go out too. If you go out once a week for food and drinks, it wouldn't be unreasonable to think you would spend about $600/mo on food and drinks. Down to about $1500/mo now.

Oops, your doggie ate a poisonous mushroom while you were taking her for a walk, needing an emergency vet trip and medicine. Oops, you go to start your not-so-new car and nothing happens, when you're already late for work. If you haven't realized it yet, every month of "adulting" brings you a nice surprise. Whether it's a sick pet, your car needs an alternator, your old college buddy needs to make bail...whatever the case, every month is a nice surprise waiting for your checkbook. Figure on at least $500/mo of "surprises" each month, and we're down to a whopping $1000.

"A grand, Elio? A measly grand? I toiled, I over-caffeinated, I sacrificed, and at times I may have cried a bit while trying to get through PA school... and you're telling me after all of that I may have 1000 bucks left over at the end of the month?" Look, guys, I'm going to give it to you straight. You will make good money as a PA, 6 figures is good money. It's not fantastic money, it's not sitting on a beach sipping mimosas every week kind of money, but it can give you a beautiful lifestyle if you manage it well. While the numbers above will be different for you, the important part is what's left over.

That remaining $1000 is where the magic is... sure you can spend it on luxury items and consumables, or you can take at least a large chunk of that and start investing. Wealth and growth-minded individuals know the key to financial independence at some point in time in the future will depend primarily on how and where you choose to invest in the present. There is not enough room in this book to go over all your investing options, and many of you will be exposed to it even on a peripheral level through your employer offered 401(k) retirement plans. That's a great start, but the reason I bring all this up is that I need you guys to understand that you are 100% responsible for your financial well-being.

Once you take full responsibility for your finances, and your wealth creation, you have no one else to blame at the end of the month if you don't even have $20 to put some gas in your tank. The whole point is that now that you've graduated, making a salary, and see how quickly that 6 figure salary can be whittled down, perhaps for the first time in your life, you have to start looking at money management and wealth creation more seriously. So, educate yourself on finance, start reading books, start talking to smarter people about finance, get with a financial advisor and do the things necessary to set your best foot forward for developing a life of abundance and prosperity. Once you get the money situation ironed out, life becomes dramatically more peaceful if you allow it.

Don't forget, we have already previously discussed a few different ways to make some additional money once you've graduated, and started building some experience under your belt. Again, moonlighting, taking call, working urgent care or ER shifts... once you have the degree, you can earn as much money as you can comfortably handle. Remember to keep a balanced life, I know the money is nice when it starts coming in, but don't sacrifice your health or relationships just so that you can lease a new BMW 5 Series instead of a new Honda Accord ($850/mo versus $290/mo as of this writing)!

6
___

STRAIGHT TALK

Healthcare in the US is in a bit of trouble guys. It is not a wonderful utopia where all the right things happen all the time. I'm sure you've been exposed to multiple situations during your rotations where you disagreed with some outcomes, the patient died when they didn't have to, mistakes were made, the surgery went wrong, you name it... we spend a tremendous amount of money every year on healthcare in this country, and yet our outcomes stink.

When you compare us to other high-income countries like Australia, Canada, Germany, Norway, Sweden, and the UK, we spend nearly twice as much on healthcare as they do, and yet we have the lowest life expectancy and the highest suicide rates among them. On top of that, we have the highest chronic disease burden and an obesity rate that's double the average for those countries! Don't believe me? Look it up! Clearly, we do not have everything figured out, despite our medical pride. I don't tell you this to frustrate or sadden you about your future role in this healthcare landscape. I tell this to you so that you are aware of just how important you actually are. If there is one shining light in all of this healthcare madness, I do believe it's the PA profession.

Of course, we need Physicians, we can't do what we do unless they do what they do. However, Physician salaries are not shrinking, and everyone is aware of the blossoming Physician shortages. If a PA can provide a high level of comparable care akin to their Physician counterparts, at a fraction of the cost, and be available more quickly to the healthcare system, then perhaps as the next decade or two rolls on we will start to see more significant improvements in our outcomes. I do believe that getting people access to the care they need, and doing that in a timely fashion, is a role the PA is uniquely well suited for. And this comes at a time in our country where we need this the most, especially post-pandemic. We hear the term "front lines of healthcare" thrown around by the media regularly, well it really is a battle out there. You as a PA will begin your soldiering day 1 of your new job...fighting the good healthcare fight. Although your motives will be pure, the battle rages on.

I wish I could tell you that as you prepare for PA battle, everyone will warmly receive you. I wish I could tell you that all your patients will be overjoyed when you walk into the room. I wish I could tell you that because you're a PA it will be easier. Unfortunately, I can't tell you any of those things. The most real thing you're going to receive in this book is that because you've chosen to be a PA, it will be harder. It's harder because some patients won't know what to make of you, it's harder because other people in the healthcare landscape don't think you're qualified. It's harder because our profession is still pretty young.

The good news is, however, that as awareness and appreciation of the PA profession grows, so does that of the patients towards us, and our ability to care for them improves further. Is it still a struggle? Absolutely. I have had many days of struggle because of something a patient said to me, or perhaps they just refused to see me. I could probably go on for hours about difficult patient interactions that have led me nearly to tears. I've had to take these experiences and remind myself that none of it is personal and that the patient didn't walk into the office or hospital that day and say "I'm going to give this PA a hard time!" Well actually, sometimes that does happen! But the fact remains, you conquer the doubts others have about your ability and qualifications with knowledge. You destroy the insecurity patients have by showing them how capable you actually are. You cannot get there right out of school though, you have to earn that path by taking the time, and continually applying learning on a regular basis until you feel confident in your day-to-day workings as a PA.

I know exactly what you're thinking... "And just how long does that take Elio?" I know, because I asked the same questions. At my first job as a PA, I asked that question to a PA who had been practicing for about seven or eight years, and when she told me that she didn't feel comfortable in her daily role until after about a year, I nearly gasped. I thought to myself, "I have to wait for a year before I get comfortable doing what I'm doing?"

Well, you may have to! It depends on how much you continue to pour into yourself and your patients daily. Everybody wants to leave work and unwind, you might want to go to the gym, meet some friends, maybe play with the kids...but after all of that, you have to remember that the patients will be there in the morning. You still have to figure out what's going on with them. And sometimes those decisions to act will be very difficult, even with all the additional information. For me, I found that taking 30 minutes or so after dinner to read about the day's case or patient that stumped me, really helped me to quickly improve my overall knowledge base. After about six months of doing this, I felt pretty good. But after about a year, I felt pretty strong. So do what feels natural to you, but just do it. Sometimes you won't even need 10 or 15 minutes to review some things in the evening. Whatever it takes, just do it. You will be dramatically better for it, and your patients will have better outcomes because you've continued to invest in yourself.

Again, healthcare is far from perfect, and often times it is those at the bedside who inherit much of the systemic dysfunction. You will grow broad shoulders in medicine, and feel at times that the whole thing will fall apart if you take a day off or leave on time. Remember, you're in this for the long term. Your mental health is of the highest importance. You can't single-handedly fix all the issues in healthcare, but you can be one bright light doing your best. So don't lose focus of what's important as you get out there, and see not all the dysfunction, but of all the good you can do one patient at a time.

7

OVERCOMING

Well guys, lights just came on for last call, and our time for this round is just about up. In the preceding pages, I hope you have found at least one or two bits of wisdom that you can use and apply to your professional life moving forward. I had to earn those bits of wisdom the hard way, and I hope that in giving them to you like this, your career and profession can advance more quickly and more smoothly than mine ever could. Sir Issac Newton famously said, "If I have seen further, it is by standing on the shoulders of giants."

There's no sense in reinventing the wheel for most things in your life, just simply watch, listen, and learn what has worked or failed for others before you. You can save yourself a tremendous amount of time and difficulty by absorbing this wisdom and making it your own. On a personal note, I'll say that I wouldn't change the "how" I came to be here with you today, and I'd be remiss if I didn't tell you the "why"....

One of the most pivotal moments of my life occurred during a PA school interview that went terribly wrong for me. Little did I know at the time, that brief exchange would have a tremendous impact on my life. I remember being so extremely prepared for that particular interview, I felt very confident in my ability to secure a spot in that program. I had done the homework, I knew what there was to know about the program: I knew the players, I knew what their ideal candidate looked like, and I had a strong GPA and a wealth of previous healthcare experience. Basically, I was ready to rock the socks off that interview.

So, once I arrived at the interviewing area, I was led into the empty room where the interview would take place and sat down at the requisite large wooden table. I sat quietly for a few minutes reviewing some notes in my mind about putting forth a successful interview, but felt relatively at ease and cheerful. I didn't have to wait for long before there was a knock at the door, and standing in the doorway a moment later were the Program Director and two assistants.

Still standing there motionless, she introduced herself without a smile. She had barely stepped into the threshold of the doorway when she uttered five words that changed my life. The words were so visceral, so violating, so hurtful... I was completely unprepared for them. Prior to her stepping in, I was like a bright shining balloon sitting in that office, full of eager anticipation and positivity...but her words came at me as if she wielded a spear. Deflated and disarmed by them, I was cut down to the knees in a moment. It's because of those five words that I stumbled through whatever was left of the interview after that, and blew my opportunity for PA school that application cycle. It would be 2 years before I had the nerve to reapply to PA school. Those five words were "What are you doing here?"

I can't tell you exactly what happened for the rest of that interview, because I have blocked it out. But I'm not ashamed to tell you that once I left the interview that afternoon and made my way back to my apartment, the moment my apartment door closed I was a sobbing mess. Even now, I'm fighting back tears. Why? Probably because I was not only convinced that this was my pathway, I was convicted of it. I had such clarity on the matter, but with five little words, she introduced so much doubt and skepticism into my world, that I was unable to recover.

I realize now that there was a fragility to me back then that she unintentionally exposed. Almost as if she unscrewed the lid off of me, took a quick look inside, and suggested my insides weren't good enough. To this day, I'm not entirely sure why she opened the interview the way she did, there must've been something about me or my application she simply didn't care for. Perhaps it was her standard opening line... I'll never know. Whatever her reasoning, she introduced the element of my unworthiness in her program, and simply equated me with being unfit, unqualified, and unprepared for being a PA. To say I was devastated is putting it mildly. Now, I had already had unsuccessful interviews before this one, but it was those particular words in that particular office that cut me open that day.

Unfortunately, I let her get to me...I know that now. I thought about that woman and those words for a very long time, which is why it took me two years to attempt getting into PA school again. As I told you in the beginning, it was no cakewalk getting in for this guy, and she was simply one part of a series of unfortunate incidents that made me question whether or not I should even go to PA school anymore. And that's primarily why I bring this up.

You see, I know for most of you there will be doubts, and you will question yourself. You may have family or friends that support you in your decisions, or you may have people all around you telling you what a dumb idea this or that has been. I had to eventually stop caring what other people's perspectives or opinions were in my life both personally and professionally. Why? Because that which is put in you is for you, and the reason why other people can't see it is because it was not put in them, it's not for them. People can't see what's not for them.

So there was something inside of you that put you on the pathway through PA school and now you're here. Let my humiliating experience be a lesson to you all, in that the journey is yours to take. No one else's, they have theirs, you have yours. You will continue to have experiences moving forward that will consistently introduce an element of doubt, fear, and questioning in your mind. The most important thing you can do for yourself both professionally and personally is to just not listen. That also happens to be the most challenging thing to do. Do not let the workings of the mind destroy the gifts and dreams that are within you. I temporarily allowed her doubts about me to take away the dream that was put in me. But you know what guys? The dream still found a way to get out.

That which is within you, that which you are destined to do, will find its way to your reality one way or another. This is a universal truth, there is no other way. However, while it makes its way out, you will have many many experiences and people that will try to manipulate or change that which is within you. Do not allow yourself to be victimized by these experiences. Use them to your advantage, stay true to the gifts and dreams that have been placed within you, and remember that if you only walked your journey on sunny days, you would never arrive at your destination.

All these years later, that experience still evokes a twinge of pain in me, a reminder to give myself grace and forgiveness for being human. Ultimately, I am grateful for the experience for it provided me the opportunity to look inside at a time in my life when I needed to the most. I restarted my application process two years later, and subsequently got accepted into the program of my choice. I got through PA school maintaining an average grade of 93 on all exams, received an award at graduation for consummate academics and professionalism, and scored the equivalent of a 95/100 on the PANCE. Maybe I was supposed to be a PA after all?

In an interesting twist to the story, many years later that program Director would be seeking a medical leadership position at the same hospital system I was employed with at the time...she needed a job. Unfortunately for her, I happened to be very well-known and respected within that organization. As candidates were being reviewed for the position, I was one of the PA staff that was queried for my opinion of the candidates being considered. I immediately recognized her name and credentials on the folder in front of me, and softly said to myself "What are you doing here?" I smiled and simply suggested that perhaps that particular candidate may not be the best fit for the organization. She subsequently was passed up for the position based on my input, and I have not heard anything from her since. As I've come to appreciate, fate has a wonderful sense of humor, like it or not.

And so as we come to a close, and the barkeep is telling us to settle up the tab, I just want you all to understand something: I have a tremendous amount of love and respect for all of you because I remember being young and immature in healthcare. Terrified to make the wrong move, but thrilled that a dream of mine had been realized, a mountain conquered. It didn't happen the way I expected, that's for sure, and as you all can probably testify to, it rarely does.

Now as you enter this time of your professional life with the innocence and curiosity of early childhood, I know what some of you will come up against in your careers. The challenges are significant, the struggles are real. So when the patient cusses you out, or they don't make it, or their family vilifies you, or you just can't take it anymore, please remember how special you truly are. Remember how important you are to all of this, no matter how insignificant you feel that part may be. The beauty is that you are never alone in your travels in this profession. We are all together on this journey, we are shoulder to shoulder, we are PAs.

GOD BLESS YOU ALL!

AFTERWORD

On your journey along this road, there may be times when you need encouragement or just someone to talk to. Now more than ever, mental health awareness should be a priority for us all, especially for those involved with the care of others. Supporting and encouraging one another is a mission I take seriously. So please friends, feel free to reach out to me directly at *eliostonebooks@gmail.com* anytime you may need help. I personally answer all correspondence I receive.

-Elio Stone

www.ingramcontent.com/pod-product-compliance
Lightning Source LLC
Chambersburg PA
CBHW020351130626
46549CB00006B/2268